THE INSPIRATI

the
INSPIRATIONAL
TRAINER

making your training
flexible, spontaneous & creative

PAUL Z JACKSON

KOGAN
PAGE

To my family

First published in 1998 by Gower Publishing, Hants, in hardback as
Impro Learning
Published in paperback in 2001 by Kogan Page

Kogan Page Limited
120 Pentonville Road
London N1 9JN
UK

Stylus Publishing Inc.
22883 Quicksilver Drive
Sterling VA 20166-2012
USA

British Library Cataloguing in Publication Data

A CIP record for this book is available from the British Library.

ISBN 0 7494 3468 6

Typeset by JS Typesetting, Wellingborough, Northants
Printed and bound in Great Britain by Clays Ltd, St Ives plc

Contents

Foreword

This book is an important step forward in the literature of corporate training. It is a gateway to the proper interaction between the life that exists in corporations and the real lives that people live. It assumes that we are all human, all different, and capable of responding to practical situations with our whole selves. It assumes that what people think and feel privately is relevant to how they perform on the job.

It backs up those assumptions with tools to demonstrate their reality – a rich panoply of exercises, stories and wise reflections about the nature of training and learning in a rapidly changing society. The book is designed to increase the repertoire of trainers, both experienced and inexperienced, as they approach the wide variety of practical situations in business and organizational settings.

In the old industrial model of corporate activity, the individual was seen as a 'warm body', hired to carry out instructions unthinkingly. Warm bodies were interchangeable, and no one in a management position tended to be concerned with the individuals who were the lifeblood out of which the industry was built.

With the advent of the Information Age, which has now been followed, many think, by the Age of Relationships, it became increasingly evident that the people who exist in the workplace are important in and of themselves, and not randomly interchangeable with others. For one thing, the expense and complexity of developing effective employees is now far beyond what it was in the age of industrialism. Anyone with even a modicum of responsibility must understand his or her relationship to the whole operation and must develop some particular part of the whole that is not shared elsewhere. Management ultimately depends on the integrity with which each employee performs.

Nowadays there is increasing concern about the need to train people who are capable of carrying out the jobs that need doing. We are, indeed, approaching a time (if we have not already reached it) when it will simply be impossible to staff certain operations with adequate workers, as they are not available. As they say, 'Good help is hard to find'. Yet we are all 'help', and we must all, therefore, increase our capacities to be more helpful to each other.

This means that, whether they like it or not, the world's leading corporations will find themselves in the education business. But what kind of education business will they be in? In the old model of education, like the old industrial model, the individual does not matter. Courses are designed to take people through a set of hurdles that they must overcome. Standardized tests are used to determine how well they have met them.

In the new model, by contrast, we recognize that each individual is different and has different talents. Matching the person to the job thus becomes a matter of noticing and capitalizing on those differences. As soon as we admit that individual differences are important, we must decide how they can best be developed in a group setting. We are, it has lately been learnt, creatures of many different kinds of intelligence. Howard Gardner has identified a minimum of seven of these: the logical/mathematical, the linguistic, the spatial (or visual), the bodily kinaesthetic, the interpersonal, the intra-personal and musical intelligence. You'll find the seven intelligences ably described and applied in this book.

There is only one way to educate all of these intelligences at the same time in a way that allows each person unique self-expression and that is through the technique of drama, which necessarily uses all of them in equal amounts. Drama, however, need not be thought of in terms of stage plays. The drama of life occurs every time we have an interaction with another person, and such interactions should be taking place all the time in training sessions. The effective trainer is thus a dramatist of sorts – both an actor in presenting the material, and a director in eliciting interactions from the trainees. This is an art, and the art is developed and fuelled through knowledge of a wide variety of effective approaches and theoretical considerations of the sort developed in this book.

What Paul Jackson has to offer us, then, is probably the most essential and basic ingredient of the new approach to corporate training that is beginning to emerge worldwide. Carefully he builds up the context for what he is telling us to do, by always placing it in a variety of possible corporate settings and taking into account the various problems that may arise in moving from the old model of interaction in which a trainer lectures to a group, to the new model in which those in the group discover themselves both as individuals and team members through the variety of different forms of improvisation.

I feel certain that this book will become a classic – one that every manager and everyone in the training business will wish to own as an essential part of the tool chest that we all must have, whether we are teaching people how to hang telephone wires, or seeking to promote change in a corporate culture.

While this book is aimed specifically at corporate and business settings, I am certain that it will be coveted by schoolteachers as well, for many of its techniques are just as applicable with children learning the basics as they are in corporate settings. We are all, as learners, beginners at something, and, as such, have a need to experience the wonder and delight of encountering and contemplating something new to us. In the process of considering that element of wonder, we come to an element of experience that transcends the practical aspects of learning, but is, if anything, more important.

We are spiritual beings, whether or not we visit places of worship or believe in any particular dogma. Being spiritual means simply that we value the way we interact with our fellow creatures. Only when we have the opportunity to explore those interactions through the kinds of media that Paul Jackson suggests, can we realize the yearning for a meaningful life that many of us feel, often without being aware of what is causing it.

So the use of these activities and the processes that will emerge from them can accomplish far more even than is claimed for them by the author. It is up to each of us who work in corporate training to explore them and find our own applications of them. The results, carefully nurtured, are bound to be compelling.

Peter Kline
Chairman, Integra Learning Systems
Author of Ten Steps to a Learning Organisation *and*
The Everyday Genius

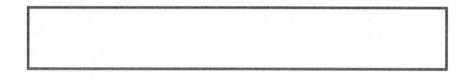

Preface

WHOSE STORY?

A visitor to a training trade fair asked me how improvisation could help him be a better trainer. Preferring to demonstrate rather than explain, I asked if he was willing to have a go. He was. Together we made up a story about a ship. We worked within a simple structure – each using one word at a time, alternating words which formed the story. Between us we told of a voyage in which the ship and its crew survived storms and piracy.

After about two minutes the tale ended and my visitor asked, 'Whose story was it?' We worked out the answer: sometimes he led, sometimes he followed. He gained insights into the subjects of taking charge and letting go. On the basis of this story-telling experience, we discussed leadership skills. He realized that there were benefits here for trainers, and introduced himself as a publisher.

This book is a direct result of that meeting. I can also trace its origin to a BBC management training course five years earlier, in which participants were offered a chance to take over the course for a day and share skills with each other by leading some of the sessions.

COMEDY

At the time I was a senior producer in Light Entertainment, making comedies and quizzes for the BBC radio network and for several years I had been teaching drama and improvisation to performers who applied their talents to the stage, radio and television. I knew that some of the techniques and skills were accessible to non-performers as I had learnt them myself as a shy amateur. And I knew they were fun to try. The essence of improvisation is spontaneity, and spontaneity usually generates laughter.

So I organized a session for the BBC course's assortment of location managers, graphic designers, accountants and producers. We used warm-ups, team exercises, trust games and role-plays, many of which are familiar to theatre students, but were a revelation to the middle management of the BBC.

Not only were the processes enjoyable, they proved to be useful. Clearly, these sessions were a refreshing way for managers to develop their present-ation skills, communication, creativity and teamwork. The time had come to combine Stanislavski with Charles Handy.

Since then, I have developed the techniques of rehearsal, performance and improvisation and applied them in many organizations. Apart from drama, I have drawn inspiration from sources including Accelerated Learning, Neuro-Linguistic Programming (NLP), the Alexander Technique, sports psychology and many management writers and practitioners.

CONTEXTS FOR INSPIRATION

The Inspirational Trainer is designed for use in a wide variety of training contexts. My own experience ranges from one-hour motivational sessions, through half-day workshops on teambuilding and one-day courses in sales and negotiations to week-long events on managing change. Some training programmes are sustained over two to three years.

It is possible to empower people in virtually any encounter. We can always listen, empathize and support. Both parties may learn. Training could be defined as any experience where we have deliberately structured a prospect of learning taking place.

Many organizations are demanding more flexibility of their members, and almost anyone can find themselves assigned a role in which they have to organize, present, facilitate, mentor, coach or train. The principles in this book should prove useful to anyone in these circumstances, and are equally applicable for external and internal trainers. The aim is to help trainers develop trainees' skills – in short, to enable learning.

Whatever series of events makes up a training programme, there is scope for more excitement, fun and effectiveness. Whether you prefer to run brief gadget-free courses in bare rooms, technology-laden seminars, indoor retreats or outdoor adventures, self-directed open-ended programmes or tight qualification-based modules, shop floor or boardroom events – you can improve them all with the guidelines offered here. *The Inspirational Trainer* consists of tools plus attitude.

If your needs go beyond the programmes presented in the book, there will be ways you can adapt the processes for your own purposes. In any case, the point is to make the material your own to benefit yourself and your trainees.

Should you wish to find out more about consultancy or training events, or if you would like to make comments regarding the concepts in this book, please write to me at:

Paul Jackson Associates
8 The Firs
Combe Down
Bath BA2 5ED

E-mail me at paul@impro.org.uk or visit the Web site at www.impro.org.uk

Preface to the paperback edition

This paperback edition benefits from a number of changes.

The first is the change of title from *Impro Learning* to *The Inspirational Trainer*. *The Inspirational Trainer* is a title that captures the spirit of the book. It is a good description of my favourite practitioners and is the title to which I aspire when designing and delivering training. I would like you to enjoy that quality of inspiration by using the ideas and methods in the text.

I have tidied the text to ensure that all the ideas are clear and accessible to anyone who finds themselves training, teaching, facilitating or leading a group where some sort of learning is happening. In each chapter, you will now find a box of 'Inspirations', containing the most important concepts and tips pertaining to that chapter or section topic.

And yet there are fewer changes than we might have expected a good three years on from the first writing of the material. Fashions in training may change reasonably swiftly, yet the basic principles remain sound, even with the advent of trends which appear to herald radical shifts – such as interactive computer-based training. I'm pleased to stand by all the content of the original *Impro Learning* and would like to thank the dozen or so reviewers who have praised it in print and the hundreds of book-buyers who have also endorsed its worth. I hope there will be many more who enjoy it in this paperback edition.

Acknowledgements

My thanks go to my esteemed colleagues and associates including Mark McKergow, Rob Weston, Richard Mindel, Doug Sawyer and my wife Deborah Jackson. They have each read part or all of the manuscript, so I would like to blame any remaining errors or misjudgements entirely on them.

I also wish to acknowledge the support of the clients of Paul Jackson Associates, not only for providing many of the cases explored in the text, but also for their generosity in discussing new ways of working. A thank you, too, for those who read and commented on the manuscript, and to Simon Woollaston for designing the illustrations.

My sources of inspiration are numerous. Some are credited in the Further Reading list, others include the many actors with whom I've collaborated on improvisational projects, especially Kit Hollerbach, Nelson David, Toby Longworth, Josie Lawrence and Paul Merton, Jim Sweeney and Steve Steen, Peter Wear and all the stars of *Comedy Express*, *More Fool Us* and the *Comedy Store Players*. Thanks again to them, to the fellow members of the Bristol Solutions Group and anyone I should have mentioned but haven't.

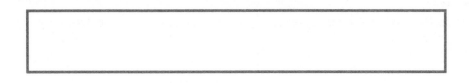

Introduction

THE CHALLENGE

The Inspirational Trainer offers you ways to bring together your own development – as a trainer and a person – with the development of participants on your programmes. Its objectives are to enable you to:

- design and deliver training programmes that provide demonstrable results by bringing out the best in participants;
- improve your skills as a platform presenter and group-leading facilitator;
- stimulate creative insights which you can apply to all aspects of your training projects;
- broaden the range of programmes you can deliver by understanding and being able to apply the principles of learning;
- increase your inner confidence, expression of confidence and ability to use your creative talents in both training and learning.

Training programmes are rehearsals for success – the successes of individuals and their organizations. As a trainer, you can help participants shape and improve their performances.

By using the tools, models, principles, ideas and attitudes of inspirational training, you give your trainees the chance to practise, absorb and learn through a method which mixes shrewd planning with great freedom and flexibility, serving the particular needs of each encounter as it unfolds.

There are many means by which you can release potential in the people with whom you work. The structured time that we call a training and development programme is pure, concentrated opportunity but, because that time is limited, we need to be excellent at what we do in order to achieve our aims. Sometimes we provide the content, at others we elicit it from participants. There are moments when control is vital, others when the art is to let go. Throughout, we require a great deal of confidence and a dash of creativity.

By starting from a confident baseline, trainers can broaden the range of contexts that they are able to handle – from powerful small groups to amazing, big events. When we train effectively, participants not only gain insights and deeper understanding of what they are doing, but also find tools to do familiar tasks better and new tasks well.

Confidence provides a foundation for creativity: when we feel secure in our methods and material, we can depart from set scripts and respond to trainees' particular needs. In this way, the work becomes more immediate, capitalizing on the advantages of live delivery over other means of training. In short, it becomes more inspirational.

As organizations become more flexible, so too does the structuring of training. Many managers across many functions are asked to deliver training alongside or even in place of specialists.

Who can be an inspirational trainer?

- full-timers;
- occasionals;
- internal consultants;
- external consultants;
- freelancers;
- lecturers;
- teachers;
- facilitators;
- academics;
- managers from the school of life;
- coaches.

Whatever our precise titles, when we take on the trainer's mantle it helps to know how people learn and what they expect from their training programmes. The first challenge is to deliver it, and beyond these basics we increasingly add inspirational value.

THE NEED FOR ADAPTABILITY

Clearly, much adaptability is demanded of everyone involved in training. But for many of us it does not come naturally.

Most people tend to follow the same sorts of pattern each time they face a similar circumstance. Being consistent makes things easier for others and for ourselves. For example, it saves time and energy to take the same route to work each day. We could call the familiar patterns a script, and we all know people who stick closely to their scripts.

Yet we do remain free to ditch the script, if we wish, and start to improvise. Taking a new route to work may prove stimulating and refreshing. Increasing our range by occasionally experimenting strengthens our ability to perform well whatever the circumstance. In my work with presenters and actors, we find it useful to move away from the idea of acting (particularly in the sense of 'play-acting', which suggests falsity and not being oneself) and work with the concept of performing (perform, from *fournir* -- to supply – and *per* – for). Improvisational techniques give actors far more power in their performances and, when applied in organizations, they empower trainers and participants too.

Improvisation tends to inspire, as it shows the trainer thinking spontaneously – importing a jolt of energy to lift the occasion from the routine. The key skill areas within which the trainer has an opportunity to inspire in this way are listed below.

Essential skills for a trainer

- analysing what makes things work well;
- creating conditions in which others can perform at their best, without fear of mistakes;
- presenting new skills or information;
- structuring the learning;
- supporting, encouraging and motivating;
- reporting back to trainees.

HOW TO FIND YOUR WAY AROUND THE BOOK

There are many ways in which my material could be ordered. All the concepts are interconnected and you may feel free to dip in anywhere, prepared to enjoy the whirlwind.

For simplicity, I have started by following the chronology of a typical training programme, beginning with a chapter identifying the sets of people which a training programme must satisfy, suggesting methods for attracting the right participants and offering guidance on outlining a course while you negotiate the brief.

By encouraging trainees to arrive in a positive frame of mind and providing a welcoming environment, you set the stage for learning, and Chapter 2 explains how to make the choices that will enable you to create the atmosphere you want.

Content is an important part of most training programmes, but the days of delivering only content are gone. Students are no longer prepared to accept boring lectures and dull handouts, and it is futile to hope that messages will automatically be received and acted upon. For many people, learning is a more dynamic process, and it is the *process* that trainers need to master. Content, while necessary, has now become secondary.

The inspirational training method concentrates on the conditions and processes of training. I describe many games and exercises, which can be adapted to incorporate a variety of subject matter.

Because activities bring content to life, they are at the heart of inspirational training. If the subject is maintaining a profitable business, we might run a 45-minute simulation of a production line, in which teams forecast their results, allocate resources, make a set of objects against a deadline and discover their profitability. This is likely to be a far richer exercise than a reading or a discussion, because participants are involved on more levels and engage their imaginations as they make meaningful choices. Taking swift decisions in the free flow of a structured process is a profoundly improvisational experience. The content – of at least those aspects of running a business – is wrapped up in the process and can be unpacked either during the game or afterwards.

Learning is encouraged by experience and by reflection. In a simulation, participants try out new behaviours, which provide material for reflection and can serve as rehearsals for future action.

Many of the games and exercises are presented here in carefully ordered sequences which draw participants in and help them reach increasingly sophisticated levels of awareness and discovery. One of the skills of this sort of training is to find apt sequences of processes, so that the cumulative effect is greater than the sum of the parts.

A sequence for activities
A sequence typically moves well:

- from simple activity to complex;
- from inward expression to outward (starting, for example, with individual planning and ending with a performance);
- from solo to group;
- from practising individual elements of a skill to a climax that encompasses all the critical components.

The sequences I describe have worked well in my experience. There will be other sequences that work as well or better, and one of the challenges for each trainer is to find them – often by making inspired on-the-spot decisions in the light of participants' responses. Also, almost any game can work out of sequence, or on its own. If it seems to fit a need or strike a chord for a particular purpose in one of your programmes, by all means use it.

Chapter 3 shows how to deploy activities to bond participants into a group. It describes some of my favourite ice-breakers and offers techniques for keeping trainees' attention on the tasks and subjects of the sessions.

MODELS AND CONFIDENT PERFORMERS

One of the benefits of inspirational training is that no one person is expected to have all the answers. While some demands on the trainer are reduced, others increase – and one of the new roles requires the trainer to be a model of certain behaviours. If we are asking participants to learn, it helps to show that we are open to learning ourselves. And that means change.

Simply by adopting the practices proposed by this book, you will be making changes, which can be a frightening prospect. Just as those you train will be asked to go through processes which they may regard with trepidation, suspicion or downright reluctance, so you face some unknowns.

You will find that once you begin the process of change, the effects are cumulative. When you do something different, reactions to you will be different. You are in new territory, which may strike you as easy, daunting or challenging, and it helps to enter it thoroughly equipped – with an overview of the terrain, a guide to the important details and a set of well-chosen tools which you know how to use.

For several years I have been devising and conducting courses and workshops in which participants have developed skills in expressing themselves with confidence, living spontaneously and rediscovering their creativity. In programmes targeted on change, they learn how to deal with uncertainty and perhaps even embrace it for the opportunities and freedoms it can bring. They also learn that freedom always has a context or structure. Jazz musicians, for example, improvise freely within the given structure of a rhythm or melody. They establish the structure, play with it, refer to it, leave it for a while and may eventually return. All of us can develop the skill of recognizing the significant structures within which we operate and find the fullest freedoms that those structures allow us for inspiring ourselves.

While jazz musicians stretch a tune and actors explore the extremes of a character, test pilots discover the capabilities of new planes by 'pushing the envelope'. Experience tells them the likely responses of the pieces of equipment, and – as Tom Wolfe describes vividly in *The Right Stuff* (1979) – the art is to encroach bit by bit into the unknown, flying the aeroplane to the limits of its safe capability, but not beyond. We can push the envelopes of our own experience in order to have fun, meet challenges and grow.

Chapter 4 analyses the concept of a trainer as an inspirational model. Expressing yourself confidently as a trainer involves performing. There are two meanings of 'performing' which are relevant to our purposes: 'putting on a show' and 'doing well'. Everything we do may be considered as a performance of some sort, and our performances are within our control. That is, we can change the way we present and conduct ourselves so that we become excellent performers.

During a training session we may need to switch from being dynamic speakers addressing the whole group to one-to-one counsellors, with the emphasis on listening. At other times, we may be infinitely flexible facilitators, doing whatever is necessary to help a process along its way.

We are probably all aware that we project different aspects of our personalities more strongly depending on circumstances – we may display one front for our parents, another for children, a third for colleagues, and even different performances for the same people on different occasions.

Chapter 5 advises on presenting yourself to advantage, particularly up-front, on the platform. While there is no single secret to developing your own or other people's skills, there are many valuable, accessible keys. One of the most useful is to understand and use the concept of leverage – how a small shift in one place brings about a big change elsewhere. Leverage – a familiar technique in many areas, from physics to finance – allows large gains from minimal investments, and this book is designed to help you to find the leverage in training. We can apply levers to our own efforts and also teach levers to our trainees.

One powerful lever is confidence itself. The same course delivered in one instance by a confident trainer and in another by someone lacking confidence will have hugely different impacts. The small matter of confidence – or the even smaller matter of the trainer's apparent confidence during a first session – often makes the difference between success and failure.

When you watch a confident trainer, you notice how they inspire confidence in trainees. It is as if the trainer's attitude has the power to carry the learner across a skill or knowledge gap. If the trainer conveys a belief that the training is going to work, the trainees draw on that to nourish their own self-belief and overcome their fears.

Circuit training

I once attended a fitness course in Cornwall – mainly to get fit, partly to observe the coach. After a young woman had climbed a gruelling set of ropes and beams in record time, the coach said to her, slightly too emphatically, 'I never thought you'd manage that'. Her confidence wilted even though her achievement was plainly visible. She had climbed beyond her expectations, and obviously beyond those of the coach, who was caught by surprise and uttered his deflating comment. It was the last time she excelled on that circuit.

Conversely, there's the effect of positive expectations. If teachers are told that their pupils are gifted and treat them as such, they respond with good results and behaviour, even if they previously scored and behaved poorly. Since Rosenthal and Jacobsen published details of their classic schoolroom experiments (1968), the power of expectation has been proved many times with students of all calibres.

As trainers, we don't need to be misled to achieve the same effect. By acting as if our participants are going to succeed, we increase the chances that they will. There are practical exercises for trainers and trainees to discover, rediscover, sustain and present confidence.

MOTIVATION, ENERGY AND SUCCESS

Chapter 6 explains how to gain co-operation and better results by understanding how to motivate participants. People change when they are ready, but they are also usually ready to respond to a vision that captures their imagination or if they can see tangible benefits from the changes proposed.

Those who attend training programmes tend to be open to exciting new ideas. They may feel they need change because of problems in their lives, problems apparent in their organizations, or simply because they realize it's time to move on. They may feel galvanized by a sense of opportunity or by realizing that change is probably a constant and that there's a lot of it around for them right now. Whatever impetus participants bring, trainers can set their sights high.

Training programmes are often a crucible for significant change. While it is true that people learn only when they are willing, the trainer is like an alchemist who determines whether the output at that instant is lead or gold.

As trainers we set the scene. Change management programmes, for example, can be described as operating on a principle of pain. Suppose that the pain level induced by current practice is 100 and that the aim of the programme is to reduce this level to 50. The transition may well mean a temporary pain level of 200. During the transition, everyone may be tempted to revert to the old ways, which are more comfortable than the current process. By providing the prospect of a quick conclusion to the cycle, the change manager can motivate participants to maintain forward progress. Ironically, trainers can help by making the starting point appear more painful than it actually is (by painting a particularly bleak picture, perhaps, and stressing its lack of sustainability).

While not all programmes are called change management, all involve management of change. The pain and relief model may give us insight into participants' states of mind at various phases and help us design processes that bring trainees through difficult transitions with a minimum of fear, disruption and real pain, and a maximum of dignity, joy and sense of achievement.

The chapter suggests it is good policy for the trainer to ask, 'What's in it for the participants?'. The trainer should also help every participant ask and answer the question 'What's in it for me?' – a question that can be split into two: what's in it for trainees during the programme? What benefits can trainees take back to their organizations?

Variety is an excellent way of keeping participants engaged, and Chapter 7 deals with the theory and practice of learning styles, presenting ways in which learning can be made easier and more effective.

In working with pacing, rhythms and contrasts, trainers must master their own energy as well as trainees'. The dimensions of energy are explored in Chapter 8, through considerations of balance and the Alexander Technique, with a holistic approach encompassing head, heart and guts.

In the martial arts, one source of leverage is to take the energy of your opponent and turn it to your advantage. A wise trainer lightens the load by using the group's experience as a prime resource. Chapter 9 explains the creative deployment of pairs, groups and plenary sessions, skillsharing and mentoring.

The strands of spontaneity are pulled together in Chapter 10, in the form of principles derived primarily from the world of drama, restated for the benefit of organizations.

The theatre also provides the familiar concept of rehearsal. In a training programme, each participant plays him or herself in the drama of their own organization. Each has a part that can be analysed, practised and performed better. The actor is the person who generally knows that part best. The trainer works like a theatre director to abstract crucial elements and help refine the performance. This is no mere metaphor. By playing out organizational scenarios – in the structured ways described in Chapter 11 – participants rehearse for success as defined by the combined visions of the organization, the trainer and the participants. It may be expressed as a mission statement, as objectives or goals.

Training resembles a rehearsal in that it is explicitly a time of preparation. The players are removed from the business arena, so mistakes are not critical and the emphasis is on learning rather than immediate achievement. However, sometimes on-the-job training and development has an immediate impact on the business and, in this case, rehearsal is equally critical. We may need to develop the technique of mental rehearsal, for example, to increase the chances of successful outcomes. We have to find ways to improve performance from one effort to the next.

Much of my focus is on live training – programmes where for the most part the trainer is in the room or the 'field' with a group of trainees. However, the principles of inspirational training apply equally to other training situations.

For the inspirational trainer, on-the-job training away from a classroom – whether at the coalface, in an aeroplane or at the office – is a manageable variant of usual practice. One-to-one training, where there is no group, just trainer and trainee, is another variant – an example where the instructor's coaching skills will be paramount.

Even computer- or Web-based training can be enlivened by addressing trainees' preferred learning styles, and by supplementing electronic sessions with human, responsive contact. The best approach is to adopt new techniques – whether or not based on technology – when they appear to have a good chance of improving what you do.

My own bias is towards training that takes account of variants, of unpredictability. With the flexibility of live-led training, each programme, course, event or session is unique and open to unexpected bursts of creativity, insight and growth – of inspiration.

LIMITS OF TRAINING

Most people can be trained fairly rapidly in activities such as driving a car, maintenance tasks, and memory-based routines, such as learning safety procedures or mathematical formulae, but when there is an artistic dimension, there is arguably a limit to the scope for training. While it is possible to train actors, writers, creators and entrepreneurs in useful techniques, the creative germ is all their own.

Inspirational training comes into its own helping participants overcome their creative blocks, or easing communication between disparate individuals. It works well when delegates share aims within a collective set-up, such as improving teamwork; where the trainer needs to unearth lessons with common denominators or repeatable elements, which each delegate will make a point of individual learning.

If we consider 'management' and 'leadership' as creative arts, the trainer's primary role is to encourage, support and perhaps synthesize lessons from the trainees' experiences. Consider the participants as talented individuals to be set on their way and applauded from time to time.

Beyond the point of competence at which the trainee is told 'You can juggle now', 'You know the safety routine by heart', or 'You are manifestly able to change a wheel', trainer and trainee enter a new improvisational realm. From here on it is essential to trust intuitive impulses and to begin operating more instinctively.

When the training does end, we are ready to deal with measurement and evaluation, and Chapter 12 considers how to complete a programme in a satisfying manner.

We have all heard the cliché that 'people are our most valuable resource'. I suspect company bosses believe this in instrumental terms – that is, they have realized productive use of people is now more profitable than productive use of machinery and land. As the value of knowledge outstrips that of older commodities, they are probably right.

However, I want to bring out the best in people because such work has a worth beyond that typically recognized by commerce or governments – even those with elevated mission statements. Enabling people to realize what they can achieve is important, creative work. It is a human value to inspire them and help provide the means for those achievements.

The case of the vanishing managers

Companies that neglect human values drain our energy. As Gareth Morgan writes in *Imaginization* (1993): 'An organisation has no presence beyond that of the people who bring it to life'. In one organization where I worked, the training department was the oasis of sanity in a desert of poor managerial practice. By providing good skills development, counselling and materials about better management, the trainers were gradually influencing the whole organization. When it failed to respond sufficiently fast or far-reachingly, many of the newly-trained managers, including me, left – more inspired than deflated.

The organization had a commitment to training and development, but one that was not harmonious with the dominant culture – the way the business was actually run. The management haemorrhage left it anaemic and struggling.

INSPIRATIONS

- More people find themselves training in more contexts. They need to be experts in process as well as content.
- Training is usefully viewed as a rehearsal for success. It works best when it is inspirational – and that means the trainer needs skills of adaptability, spontaneity and creativity.
- When organizations are receptive to learning, they flourish by developing the skills, attitudes, goals and atmospheres appropriate for modern business. And whoever designs and delivers the training has a most significant role to play.

1

How little do you need to know?

Our chronology begins with identifying the sets of people a training programme must satisfy, suggesting a winning proposal, writing the brief and attracting the right participants.

BEFORE THE BRIEF

A songwriter was asked which came first – the music or the lyrics? He replied, 'The phone call'. Trainers, in common with the songwriter, need a commission to kick-start the practice of their craft.

Landing a commission depends on making the right proposal, often in competition against other training suppliers. Even if you are an in-house trainer, you still need to sell your wares, however informal the internal market. For your work to be satisfying as well as profitable, you need to bear in mind there are at least three sets of people who want something out of a training programme:

- **The client.** The client pays for the programme and expects value for money. This might be measured against results such as identifiable effects on profits or productivity; displays of greater harmony in the workplace; safer working practices or raised morale.
- **The participants.** They want value for time spent and any effort they put in. They may share a stake in outcomes specified by clients and could be seeking a mixture of skills and empowerment. They may want certificates too.
- **The trainer.** As trainers, we want the programme to satisfy both the client and participants. We may also be aiming to achieve personal goals

through the successful running of a project: gain promotion, develop new training processes, win new business, learn from participants.

A good proposal enables all sets to be satisfied. It promises enough to offer value to the client, suggests delivery of sufficient content through attractive processes to move participants forward, and works in such a way as to reward the trainer. It also serves as groundwork for the detailed programme design that usually follows a commission.

Preparing a winning proposal

A winning proposal will:

- meet training needs;
- outline benefits for the client;
- suggest benefits for the participants;
- offer distinctive ideas about the style or the processes;
- offer something unique about the trainer.

WRITING AN INSPIRING PROPOSAL

In the excitement of discussion with a client, it can be tempting to say an unconditional 'Yes' to everything they suggest. This can be a mistake. Certainly we aim to satisfy the client, but not at the expense of the other stakeholders or if the shopping list is unrealistic. It can make more sense to say 'Yes, and that means. . .' or 'Yes, as long as we. . .'. If we need to change the constraints – of time, budget, numbers or even expectations – now is the time to do it. We should say, 'From the information I have been given, this is what it is going to take to achieve your aims. . .'.

Part of our task is to help clients understand their own requirements, at least by questioning or testing those aspects that strike us as problematic. We do this by projecting the running of the programme, reshaping it mentally to the point where we feel confident that we can deliver within an agreed framework. Here we stray into consultancy territory, in order to safeguard the integrity of the forthcoming programme.

In-house trainers and freelancers all work under constraints. Within any structure, such as the design of a training programme, you can discover the freedoms it contains. If the constraint is caused by a mismatch between what the client wants and what you are prepared to offer, that is where to

13

apply the imagination. You might, for example, need time to research a particular topic before delivering a programme. Alternatively, by checking your needs as well as those of the client and the participants, you might become alert to such possibilities as negotiating a longer programme or bringing in a specialist assistant for part of a project: 'I can provide the team-build aspects myself, and we'll appoint Richard to administer the psychometric tests'.

The winning proposal is designed to meet needs, and is worded in terms of benefits. State the improvements that will accrue to the organization and the individuals as a result of the programme: 'Participants will be equipped with a method that will enable them to sell more chips'; 'The company will benefit from raised morale'; 'Everyone who attends will be able to write a report containing the key points, without waffle. This will clarify communications, save time and avoid confusion'. What you do not need to reveal are the precise methods by which these goals will be achieved. You may already have a fair idea of appropriate processes, but you must leave yourself and your participants room to improvise during the learning period.

Finally, aim to include something unique or distinctive in your proposal. This might be a need that you alone have succeeded in articulating, a benefit offered only by your programme, or a special way of working that particularly appeals to the client. A key for finding the distinctive aspect is to discover why the client has come to you – and not to someone else. You can either ask the client directly, or ask yourself. If you discover that you are competing, the question becomes 'What will enable me to win?'.

There will always be some extra element beyond the mechanics of the assignment and this will be something that you – and only you – can provide. Perhaps the client has a sense of your particular qualities; whether you bring steadiness, excitement, reliability, strictness or tolerance, speed, invention or experience. If you were recommended, can you find out what your proponents liked about your work and what benefits their organizations gained from your intervention? Therein lies the secret of your personal inspirational qualities.

Sometimes a winning proposal can be made by telephone or during a face-to-face conversation. That's fine, but make sure you commit your understanding to paper (or screen), so that both you and the client have a record of what has been agreed. If you haven't done so at the proposal stage, then obtain a written agreement in the form of a brief.

The brief describes the training programme. If the client has agreed all that you have suggested, and neither of you has anything to add, then the brief is simply identical to the proposal. Usually there are changes. I once proposed a course on report writing which would be spread over two half-days, with the idea of participants taking advantage of the interval to write reports to provide raw material for the second session. In the end, for logistical reasons, they preferred a one-day course, and the practical writing session was condensed into a very busy lunchtime.

For each training project you will almost certainly have to generate a series of written documents. With a word-processor, it is elegant and economical to make each document serve as a starting point for the next. So the proposal is a draft of the brief, which contributes to the sign-up document, which in turn mutates into the trainer's notes and is a base for a participants' course pack. Once you are underway, you need never face the emptiness of a blank page.

In committing your understanding to writing, you can clarify discussions, tease out difficulties and make your intentions explicit.

The document sequence

1. Proposal.
2. Brief.
3. Contract or letter of agreement.
4. Your trainer notes.
5. The participants' pack.

DEGREES OF DETAIL

I have found a huge variation between clients in terms of how much detail they want in the brief. At the vaguest end, the commission is to 'pep up our sales team'. At the other extreme, there will be a list of a dozen or so closely-defined competencies and a specified outcome – for example, that each participant be rated higher in each competency at their next appraisal. Personally, I am happy with either approach, as long as we share an understanding (confirmed in writing) of the desired outcomes – what the programme is supposed to deliver.

If the client is well organized, the training will fit into a model like this:

15

A strategic approach to training

- Identify the business goal.
- Assess the personal skills/knowledge needed.
- Assess the existing capabilities.
- Meet any shortfall by training (in-house or sub-contracted).
- Monitor to ensure that goals are being met.

With other clients, training strategy may be more haphazard, perhaps governed by a traditional timetable, a sudden sense of urgency, or the whim of a managing director. The programme that you provide can still be of immense value, but there is likely to be more groundwork needed before you turn your brief into a full programme design.

A revealing question is to ask the training buyer what outcomes the participants want, as distinct from those sought by the organization. I explain that the course works by offering participants possible results which they themselves will value – otherwise they will engage with the programme only reluctantly, if at all, and are much less likely to learn or experience anything useful.

A simple tactic for obtaining a helpful list of desired outcomes is to ask your client to find out on your behalf what the participants want. Some companies will have already done this systematically as part of a training needs analysis. The lone-wolf managing director may be prompted to do so by your request.

Beware though. The weakness of training needs analyses is their lack of clarity or accuracy. People say they want certain things, and perhaps really they don't. Or by the time the training comes around they no longer want those things. Or the needs are imprecisely defined.

This, however, can be to your advantage. The inevitable degree of vagueness in the descriptions of outcomes listed in most briefs means that training programmes must remain flexible, allowing room for improvisation. Briefs are subject to many levels of interpretation, and a lack of prescription actually increases the chances of each participant getting what they want – even if it is never stated – from the wealth of possibility open to them. This is one of the key differences between a computer-based training programme that rigorously follows a syllabus, for example, and a sophisticated training course that maximizes its trainees' potentials.

An improvisational approach to training which has not been over-defined, also makes it more probable that clients and participants will obtain unexpected value from a programme. For example, it becomes apparent on many courses that there are benefits when people meet each other away from the regular routines of work. When they first meet someone who has previously been only a name on memos, interdepartmental co-operation will probably improve immediately. The value of this new relationship will be apparent to the people concerned, and may later be appreciated by the organization. Alternatively, experienced colleagues may suddenly see each other in a new light: as they each experience successes related to the content of the programme, they gain respect for each other, which will enhance their working relationship when they return to base.

These are relatively obvious added values, because any course can bring developmental bonuses for individuals and their organizations. Any evaluation of training programmes should take these hidden values into account and accept that elements of judgement are involved. It is a mistake to believe that training (or evaluation of any human process) can be reduced to financial or numerical values alone. As training researcher Eric Jensen puts it, 'Let's make what's important more measurable, rather than making what's measurable more important'.

ON-THE-SPOT BRIEFS

A trainer confident of his or her inspirational abilities can shape a proposal and design a brief during a conversation with the client. There are certain points you need to cover to obtain a feel for the job. If the client doesn't raise them, then take the initiative and make sure you discuss:

- how long the training programme will take;
- how many people can attend the programme at one time;
- what facilities are needed;
- what the training programme will cost;
- how the training is going to be evaluated.

It is good practice in quick thinking to handle these issues on the spot. You already have enough experience of training programmes to know the likely parameters. You can probably do this work accurately in an instant and need not follow the conventional practice of many training firms, which is to promise to come back with answers later. Until you feel totally confident, you can state that these are your first thoughts and you will return with a more polished proposal. By dealing with these questions as you shape the proposal, you benefit from bouncing ideas between you and the client. Remember, you will be writing a proposal or a brief anyway; this will give you an opportunity to explain why you are now revising initial suggestions.

How long will the training take?

The first step to finding the answer is always to ask how long you can have. While it is not uncommon to be asked how long it will take, I find increasingly that timescales are given, or at least intimated, by clients, rather than trainers. When this is so, the on-the-spot proposer should indicate how much progress he or she might expect to make within the time allotted.

While it is never possible to be entirely sure how long it will take to train any particular group to any particular outcome, there are some useful guidelines. College-type courses are generally designed to give enough time for each participant to achieve a required standard. Even so, people sometimes need an extra year to pass a two-year course. Most people can achieve certain safety competencies in a few minutes. We can easily teach anyone how to strap on a safety helmet for a site visit. A proposed training programme might simply be a sequence of similarly straightforward routines.

With less definable skills – such as communication, negotiation or creativity – it is difficult to be as precise, although we can quickly get a feel for desirable programme lengths. During the discussion, I find it useful to sketch out a ready-reckoner which helps estimate either an ideal running time or give a sense of how much can be incorporated into a given period.

The idea is to assign processes or exercises as the client specifies each outcome. Add up the time taken by each process and you have the length of the programme.

Ready-reckoning for on-the-spot briefs
Programme length based on outcomes mentioned by the client.

The client says: 'We are bringing together a new team of eight people, and we want them to get to know each other better, so that communication between them is open and efficient. Each of them will be leading a project of their own, and some will be new to that role'.

The trainer calculates: 'Teambuilding' > Get team to bond = two icebreakers and review. Time = 90 minutes.

This starts the teambuilding process. The greater the importance of the teambuilding element, the more processes you may need. Bear in mind that many exercises aimed at other outcomes also generate worthwhile teambuilding experiences.

'Better communication between individuals' > Simulation and debrief. Time = 2 hours.

'Development of leadership skills in eight participants' > Eight leadership opportunities in a variety of processes. (Run processes simultaneously, but minimum of 4 hours.)

Plus explanation of theory (30 minutes), presentation of models (30 minutes), action planning (40 minutes).

Minimum total time = 9 hours, 10 minutes.

In the example above, clearly a half-day course would be too short to accomplish the objectives. A one-day course would be a minimum, and would accomplish a number of valuable processes. Two days would allow time for each primary process we have in mind, with scope for reinforcing processes, proper reflection and attention to individual needs and contingencies. As required outcomes begin to multiply, we envisage a lengthier course, possibly a full week, or of single days once a week or once a month for six, eight or more sessions.

When you are running a course of one day or longer, aim to arrange a follow-up session with the same participants. Knowing there is to be a follow-up reinforces the message that actions are indeed to be taken and this brings home the importance of transferring learning into practice. When the rehearsal is over, it is time to perform. You should ask trainees to take actions based on decisions made during the programme and to notice the impacts. Then in the follow-up session, have them report on the consequences, consider alternatives and advance their action plans.

With experience, you will know what you can expect to accomplish, and will find yourself in a strong position to negotiate reasonable timescales for the outcomes required. Failing that, you can use your instant reactions to help manage client expectations.

How many people can attend the programme at one time?

One popular group size is from 8–12 people. Some of the many advantages to this size are that:

- it is large enough to encompass a range of experience and abilities;
- it is large enough to attack collaborative tasks or comparative/competitive tasks in more than one team;
- participants can be mixed into different configurations for different processes;

- it is small enough for the trainer to deliver individual coaching and feedback to everyone;
- it is small enough for everyone to have their say;
- it is small enough for everyone to get to know everyone else, but large enough to select working partnerships.

Smaller groups tend to be more intense. This can be valuable, particularly if the training is largely self-directed. For economic reasons, the small group is likely to consist of senior staff, and has proved an excellent format for resolving interpersonal issues, and for facilitated strategy sessions, including creative problem-solving.

Nevertheless, nothing in inspirational training confines the trainer to small groups. While there may be logistical difficulties with groups of larger than a dozen or so participants, there are advantages for the trainer and for economy-minded clients. If your discussion is leading you towards a large group, check that you will have the resources to work collectively and in subgroups or syndicates.

For parts of the programme where all participants are gathered together, we can inspire tremendous collective commitment to the training objectives and engender synergies between subgroups. The talent base and energy base are greater, and the impetus they generate can carry the less committed through any difficult patches by sheer inertia.

Big events can be amazing and memorable. They can inspire the imagination to create spectacle on a grand scale, perhaps building great outdoor structures. There are events where teams build bridges over chasms, drum through the night and create their own comedy sketch show (not all in the same event!).

If the client wants a short event for many people, we can still deliver effective training. People can learn from anything. And training includes any experience that you structure with particular learning in mind.

There are some simple techniques which we can use to become comfortable about accepting broader and more challenging briefs and therefore widen our range. If, for example, we specialize mainly in one-to-one coaching and small groups and feel less confident about dealing with larger numbers, we can recreate familiar conditions within bigger groups. We can deploy assistants to keep events on track. We might set up subgroups with monitors, temporary leaders or self-directing structures. Gradually we exchange the close supervision available in smaller groups for a more free-form, dynamic, self-regulating event. Although with larger numbers of people there is less scope for everyone to have as much one-to-one contact with the trainer, we can substitute systems whereby everyone has one-to-one experience in pairs – perhaps with processes featuring changing of partners.

As an inspirational trainer, you will develop the confidence to direct the group *en masse* when necessary, allow them free rein much of the time and switch appropriately between modes. With that resource, you have the scope for almost any response to the numbers question during an on-the-spot briefing.

What facilities are needed?

We shall deal with facilities, costs and evaluations in more detail in later chapters. However, at the briefing stage, you must estimate the facilities you will need for the processes you envisage. Key questions to resolve are:

- is the training to take place indoors, outdoors or both?
- is the training on-site or off-site?
- how luxurious or spartan is the venue?
- is any special equipment needed (such as vehicles, sports gear, training games apparatus; and electronic items such as videos, computers, OHPs)?

Again, check the client's assumptions – and your own. During the briefing discussion for a hotel-staff training course, it emerged that the hotel was being refurbished. I had assumed we could have our pick from a selection of grand conference facilities. As all of these were currently closed, we ended up in a bedroom! But at least checking early enough meant we had the largest room available, which I could see was just about adequate for our activities.

What will the training programme cost?

Once we have answered the above questions, the cost implications will be immediately apparent. We know roughly what we shall need to hire, and can add our professional fees (plus those of any colleagues or associates needed to perform the tasks) if we are external consultants, or delve into our time and financial budgets if we are in-house providers. A popular tactic is to present the cost of a course to a client under the heading 'Your investment'.

How is the training going to be evaluated?

It is wise at the briefing stage to at least test the waters of evaluation, perhaps by floating our own ideas of how we might like to assess the training. Concentrating on benefits, outcomes and an appreciation of value for money will help maintain our enthusiasm as we describe the heady hour of challenges we are about to set our 500 participants in the name of improved leadership skills.

BEYOND THE BRIEF

As the proposal crystallizes into the brief, we are already thinking ahead to the design of the programme, which can be documented in two sets of notes – one for the trainer(s) and one for participants. We have agreed outcomes with the client, committed practical parameters to paper and have a good idea of course content and processes.

To set the stage for inspirational training, the trainer prepares a set of notes – perhaps a series of headings, perhaps a more detailed script, which will guide the running of the event. In composing these notes, we are likely to go beyond the specified brief, with additional outcomes in mind. We can make our own assumptions about what is wanted. Although they need not be shared explicitly with clients or participants, they are a way of reminding ourselves of our own values, enabling us to place the programme in a wider perspective.

For example, we might require any training that we offer to meet certain ethical, professional or environmental standards. These could be stated in codes of conduct by professional bodies or may be our own. I know one trainer who ensures that his work remains consistent with his values by refusing any assignment that he cannot reach by public transport.

The training that I encourage is holistic, in that it aims to reach out to all aspects of the participants, and not reduce them to machine-like dimensions. The practical consequences of such a commitment include programmes with a fair amount of physical activity, music and time to express feelings. The specific additional outcomes you design are based on prior knowledge and your intuition about the particular project.

Prior knowledge

From previous experience we know that people generally want the following during a training programme:

- to be treated with respect;
- to start from where they are now – in terms of knowledge, skill or attitude;
- not to look foolish;
- to be supported and challenged;
- to enjoy the training – which requires them to find ways to participate and be committed;
- predictability;
- to be surprised.

If they experience these things during our training, then we will be going a long way towards bringing out the best from our participants. These are the elements that need to underlie our approaches to gaining the more explicit outcomes.

Whatever we learn about successful training can be incorporated into the design. Imagine, for example, that we are running a course for individuals – perhaps all from separate organizations – and that all the desired outcomes are individualistic. Nonetheless we know that they will need to work to some degree as a team, albeit temporarily, in order to gain individual knowledge and skills. While there may be no point in stressing that we are teaching team skills, we still have to impart some teambuilding simply to encourage the group to work together. At the very least, mutual support will buttress each individual's learning.

Intuition

Intuition is an underused tool for trainers to help others obtain the maximum benefit from training programmes. You can use it to enhance design by examining a bare outline of a programme implied by the specified outcomes, then adding whatever you feel is needed to make it a really good course. The chances are that this is exactly what was wanted, but not stated, by the client or participants.

My intuition often tells me to include the opposite of the current mood of the client organization. For a traditional, serious banking client, I incorporate playfulness. Participants remember that certain ways of doing things can be fun, and they bring a new lightness into their work, which improves their communication with colleagues and customers. The client doesn't specify 'more laughter in the office' as an outcome, so that aspect of a better atmosphere is a bonus.

One route to tapping into your intuition is to imagine a part of one of your programmes unfolding with outstanding success. Notice any characteristics of the scene that have not been covered by your discussions to date. These are the parts to build into the design.

Some results of your intuitive processes may always remain covert; others you may be able to express in the brief, mentioning 'added value' and pinpointing them for evaluation.

SIGNING UP RECRUITS

Now that the course is commissioned and the design is taking shape, there is an early opportunity to gain commitment towards the project through selecting the right candidates. While voluntary attendance is usually preferable, there are some exceptions. With time management courses, for example, it is ironic that the people who will most benefit often believe themselves too busy to attend. Other programmes succeed only when top management attend in person, to show their own commitment. In these instances there is good reason for participation to be compulsory – although the blow can be softened by a clear explanation of reasons and benefits. Then, ideally, participants will see joining as a privilege and, if the client has identified training needs accurately, our programmes will be fully subscribed.

When people are sent for training – if they arrive at all – they are often unwilling and cynical. Ways of dealing with this are detailed later. For now, recognize that people learn only when they are ready to do so and that it is the trainer's task to do whatever is necessary (whether planned or spontaneously) to create favourable conditions. Take any early opportunity to give 'conscripts' the impression that they are volunteers, thereby paving the way and setting the right tone long before the programme begins. A neat way to achieve willing trainees is for the client or trainer to circulate a sign-up document (see boxed example on page 25).

In this instance, a local authority wanted to train people to work fearlessly and with commitment through a period of uncertainty. The sign-up document generated enough candidates for several courses. Notice how it incorporates elements from the proposal, brief and design, worded in such a way to appeal to individuals.

Interestingly it turned out that the participants' aims diverged from the clients'. The participants (predictably) were keen to look after themselves – to the extent of leaving the council if it suited them. If we had stressed the organizational outcomes more strongly, emphasizing, for example, motivational techniques to keep already stressed staff up to speed, the sign-up might have had less appeal.

Even the most elegant advertisement will fail to win a response if prospective candidates feel that there is nothing in it for them. The managing director of a computer systems company unilaterally decided there was a need to train his 20 senior managers to enable the company to survive a period of rapid change. He told me what he wanted; I designed a programme and sent a sign-up leaflet. The sign-up was voluntary, and not enough people volunteered. I had worked on the basis of what the MD described, which was radically different from what his managers felt was needed. This diversity was so great, and so apparent, that the programme – although booked and with a deposit paid – never took place.

A big advantage of a voluntary sign-up is that it informs the trainer whether or not there's a good match between what is on offer and what candidates want. If you cannot have volunteers, and still suspect there may be a mismatch, another option is pre-programme interviews, which, although time-consuming, reveal a wealth of information.

Beyond broad generalities, it is risky to assume that we know what participants want. Sometimes we simply have to wait until they arrive to discover their real objectives. Eventually, though, we can incorporate their needs with those of the client, honour our own integrity and design programmes that will deliver most impressive outcomes.

Sample sign-up document

Managing Uncertainty

A two-day course, with a one-day follow-up one month later.

Each course will involve 12–15 participants, from a selection of directorates.

This course is designed to provide a tool-kit for officers of the council facing the transition to a unitary authority.

In times of change, events are often unpredictable. We don't necessarily know who will have jobs, who we will be working for, who will be working for us or what our roles may be. Meanwhile, we are aiming to offer a seamless transition, delivering services to the public, despite increasing workloads. In these circumstances it is easy to feel insecure and overworked, and we need tools for dealing with stress and uncertainty.

Objectives

To manage uncertainty successfully, the manager needs:

Personally

- a well-developed sense of self;
- clear priorities;
- flexibility, including an ability to re-frame;
- the ability to remain calm and relaxed;
- sufficient support systems/structures/resources;
- skills in making the best out of any situation.

As a team member

- leadership skills – including the ability to make decisions in difficult circumstances;

- followership – empathy;
- the ability to support staff;
- the ability to motivate, delegate and ensure that work still gets done;
- good communication skills;
- strategies to combat rumour.

The course uses games, exercises, recalling, sharing, discovery, planning, goal-setting, implementing and reviewing. It is participative, practical, demanding and fun.

INSPIRATIONS

- Design your brief to satisfy the client, participants and trainer.
- Word your proposals in terms of benefits, and include what is distinctively inspiring about you.
- Use your intuition to find ways to add value.
- Design your proposal on the spot, then put it in writing.

2

Setting the stage for learning

By encouraging trainees to arrive in a positive frame of mind, and providing a welcoming environment, we set the stage for learning and can open with the impact of our choice.

JOINING INSTRUCTIONS

It's the first day. Everyone arrives in good time, relaxed and alert. There is a palpable sense of anticipation. These people are eager to try things; they are willing to learn.

And, chorus the old-school training cynics, pigs might fly! The cynics have a point. From primary school lessons to training sessions – especially if they are compulsory – learners are likely to be reluctant. If trainees feel like recalcitrant schoolkids, they will confront instructors with an impressively unhelpful battery of tactics, from apathy to contrariness, subtle sabotage to open rebellion.

Of course, some may have heard that modern training can be fruitful and fun. Much depends on the culture within their organizations, over which the trainer has little control. If participants have had poor experiences in the past, they are entitled to be suspicious about the future.

But trainers wield a fair amount of influence, and it pays dividends to encourage learners to arrive in the right frame of mind. Good preparation leaves us free to concentrate on the main thrust of the course and to increase the spontaneous inspirational aspects. Everyone's purpose is already clear, and we are able to avoid the quibbles and concerns that sap the confidence and energy of trainers and participants alike.

We discussed the idea of voluntary sign-up in Chapter 1. Whether or not that has happened, we can do more to encourage our trainees to look forward to our programmes. Our advance communications are an opportunity to:

- excite the trainees;
- set high expectations;
- prepare trainees to work hard;
- clarify objectives.

We can indicate an appealing professionalism by:

- providing clear joining instructions, including a map that covers all reasonable forms of transport to programme locations;
- being personal – it is a welcoming touch to be addressed by one's own name;
- including a contact name and number for any pre-programme questions.

We may go further, by including a small amount of work to be done before a live course begins. This could be an amusing questionnaire, psychological profile forms, or something intriguing and a bit different – such as a request to bring certain items to the first session. Avoid overload. Unless you suspect your candidates are avid bookworms, include reading lists for background information only.

Pre-course work carries certain risks: you start with a sense of failure if no one does it; candidates may do different amounts, and those who did little – perhaps feeling that the programme needs to justify itself before they put in their effort – arrive at a disadvantage compared with those who did more.

It is better to provoke thought, prompt reflection and create an expectation of a professional, interesting project. By setting the right tone at this stage, the programme will be perceived as fun, demanding, exciting, enigmatic or life-enhancing. It's up to you.

Joining instructions: Friendly

Dear David

We're delighted that you will be joining us on Wednesday 17 and Thursday 18 May for the 'Communicating' course.

Coffee is served from 9.30 am, and the first session is at 10 am. Lunch and refreshments are all provided, and we finish each day by 6 pm.

The venue is The Management Centre, London Road, Warmley, Bristol. Telephone 01179 677807. The best way to get there is either by taxi from Bristol Temple Meads or Parkway, or by car. As you know, by car, you're aiming for the A420 between Kingswood and Wick. The Management Centre is within 100 yards of two pubs, The Rose and Crown and The Griffin, set on two mini-roundabouts on the A420. From the mini-roundabouts, turn left 100 yards later into Church Road, and the entrance is on your right.

You'll be given full timetables and course packs when you arrive. You should dress comfortably.

If you have any questions, please contact me on 01225 834359. Otherwise, we look forward to seeing you at the venue.

Yours sincerely

Joining Instructions: Cryptic

The course begins in HQ training centre, room B, at 9 am on Monday 12 October. Please complete the enclosed questionnaire and bring three photographs.

If motivation might be an issue, quote from previous satisfied participants or include stories of how predecessors have succeeded. Sometimes it is valuable to contact each participant in advance by telephone or email. We may need to discover each person's experience of the subject. On a course entitled 'Advanced Facilitation', a colleague discovered through pre-course conversations that hardly anyone had any experience of facilitating. As a result, we kept the flattering title and planned our sessions to take account of their beginner status. A pre-emptive phone call gives us an opportunity to deal with fears, rather than hope against the odds that worried participants will take the initiative to call us.

PRACTICAL CONCERNS

The location of a training event will influence the atmosphere significantly. If part of the purpose is to break away from routine practices and routine thinking, it makes sense to hold the event away from the regular workplace.

Simply calling a workshop an 'Awayday' may be enough to refresh the thinking of participants. The BBC Radio Light Entertainment department liked to hold Awaydays at the seaside, within view of Victorian piers. The nostalgic reminder of our end-of-the-pier predecessors set the scene for stimulating debate on how to enthrall the modern audience.

An alternative is deliberately to hold the event in the regular workplace and begin with processes which break rules and expectations about what goes on in this setting: 'Here's the production line. Now what could be radically different?'.

Beware plush country house hotels, where participants may spend more energy digesting heavy meals and investigating the facilities than grappling with the organization's problems. The luxury setting may be more appropriate for a reward or celebratory event where learning is a secondary concern. If the venue is too bleak, however, delegates may be in no mood to learn anything other than how best to deal with adverse conditions. Admittedly, this can be a good metaphor for some organizations, which may account for the popularity of the more gruelling outdoor challenge type of training events.

There are benefits in choosing a more imaginative venue, such as a theatre, a ship, a zoo, a stately home, art gallery or museum, a TV or radio studio. The arena will then lend itself to certain activities which can be integral to the course. Whatever is unusual or unexpected will stimulate participants.

Wherever the training takes place, someone has made a choice, and that choice has impacts which will communicate themselves to participants – from first impressions through to the ambience which will pervade the entire programme.

Hotel conference facilities are safe and usually dull. They will often prove adequate, but any inspiration will have to come from the people, not the location. What is important is to avoid hotel rooms with windows that cannot be opened, thermostats that fail to work and flickering fluorescent lights. As a minimum, make sure that everyone has regular access to fresh air and natural light. This shows trainees that we are respecting their basic needs. They'll also appreciate somewhere pleasant for outdoor exercise, and anything conducive to feelings of freedom during breaks.

PREPARING THE ENVIRONMENT

If training is to be of maximum benefit, the environment is as important as the processes or contents of the programme. First, the atmosphere must be welcoming. This was the basis of Maria Montessori's philosophy for nursery education, and it revolutionized small children's pre-school lives.

We can personally greet people as they arrive, or – if we need or prefer to be elsewhere – make sure that they are met by associates. There's an advantage in saying 'hello' personally. It reduces the trainee's feelings of vulnerability and can establish a good one-to-one relationship at the outset by treating each guest uniquely, and offering a first chance to remember names when there's not too much else going on. However, the benefits can be outweighed if you dislike engaging in small talk or wish to preserve your mystique. Grand lecturers make an appearance. Matey sports coaches start with a handshake. Questions to ask if the balance is unclear are:

- What would you prefer if you were a participant on the course yourself?
- Are you going to be primarily a presenter (distant, authoritative)?
- Or will you be mostly a facilitator (approachable, accommodating)?

Put up a 'welcome' poster that tells everyone they are in the right venue. When numbers were fewer than 16, I used to include everyone by name on a simple flip-chart poster, because it had made a good impression on me when I was included in this way on a presentation skills programme. However, make sure you have the same number of names as participants, so no one is forgotten and offended. Unless the programme is administered with supreme efficiency, I now think the risks of offence through missing someone out or even a slight misspelling outweigh the benefits. Also, on some programmes, participants may consider it an over-familiarity to see their first names written up on the board, and might prefer a badge written at the time of arrival so that spellings and degrees of formality can be checked and respected.

Another possibility is a blank flipchart for everyone to sign in their individual way as they arrive – in the style of 'What's My Line?'.

Flowers and plants bring life to the sterility of so many locations, and aromatherapy has its uses – although it can be tricky to dissipate strong smells.

Check the acoustic of the room before the event. A simple way to do this is to clap your hands and listen for the echo. If the echo is crisp and clean, you are in a resonant room that will give your voice a bright, 'live' sound. Where the echo is muffled and quiet, the room is 'dead', possibly because of heavy carpeting and wall hangings. Your voice will be swallowed in such a room and it will be much harder to make yourself heard. An audience in a room will tend to absorb sound, so a very lively room is fine if you're expecting a large audience. A dead room will put a strain on your voice, and you should arrange amplification or swap rooms. I often find switching air-conditioning off after everyone has settled produces noticeably better acoustics.

Music sets the mood. Any music helps the first arrivals feel less isolated, and later there are more sophisticated ways to use it. It is an ancient method for assisting learners, dating back at least as far as Archimedes, who played music to wake his students in the morning and soothe them later in the day. More recent scholars, such as Bulgarian psychologist Georgi Lozanov, have found that certain specific uses of music improve memory retention. For the moment, consider how you can employ music as people are arriving to continue creating the impression begun with the advance communications. Classical is a safe choice for most sessions, while up-beat rock can be a perfect scene-setter for motivational events. Film music is often strongly atmospheric. I once used a raucous jazz track, of which a new entrant demanded 'What's this rubbish?', which marked the start of an excellent, if fiery, relationship. Within reason, and bearing in mind that many people have an aversion to country and western music, select something which you like personally and which puts you in the right mood for the start of an event – and there's a good chance it will have a similar impact on the participants.

Refreshments are essential. As we shall discover, events should feature frequent breaks, and people need a supply of water. However, if you only provide water, delegates tend to ask for other drinks, so it is a good idea to furnish regular tea, coffee and biscuits. Good quality biscuits make a favourable impression disproportionate to their cost. Remember also that health matters to many people, particularly as they might be contemplating their eating habits during a training session (if it's anything to do with improving lifestyles), so provide fruit and herb teas alongside the traditional caffeines and sugars.

Better refreshments help to bring out the best from trainees. While it may take a while for health benefits to manifest themselves, at least participants' confidence will be boosted by their awareness of your concern for their comfort. If effort is put in, they will tend to feel worthy of it.

The same reasoning applies to the choice of seats and desks. If you can influence the selection of chairs, aim for comfort – particularly good back support – without decadence in the form of soft cushioning.

Room layout

Consider the layout of the chairs. Straight rows suggest an old-fashioned lecture, which might be a comforting way to start for a conservative group. However, if you are taking a more facilitative approach, the group will be easier to handle if seated in a circle or horseshoe. It is always worth taking the edges off rows, even in crowded lectures, by turning every chair to face the lecturer. I insist on the proper placement of every chair for a lecture, training session or theatre show, partly to ensure that everyone seated has the best and most comfortable view available (which reduces strain and tension), and partly to help the audience focus on the speaker or performers.

To understand the significance and power of layout, consider your favourite theatre space. All the principles of theatre apply to those parts of training programmes when there's a presenter delivering material to an audience or anything significant is happening up-front. If, as a presenter, you think of your lecture sessions as theatrical shows, and you can work out the needs of the audience for this particular performance, you will be on the right lines. If, for example, you plan to walk from table to table, you can afford a far more haphazard layout than if you are going to present from a podium.

For sessions where slides, films or flipcharts are the most important elements, have the focus on them. This frees you to stand to the side, out of the limelight, or to wander about if that's what you prefer.

It is useful to know, when considering layout, that it is generally advantageous to ask participants to switch places – and quite possibly move their chairs – from time to time within and between sessions.

On one course for paintshop supervisors in a large motor company, the participants ensconced themselves behind a barrier of desks. This was what they expected in their own training centre, and they clearly were not planning to emerge in a hurry. As external consultants – guests in their habitat – we allowed them to stay behind the desks until they felt entirely safe and comfortable with the processes that we were using. After lunch on the first day, we intercepted them by placing ourselves between them and the desks, and suggested we do a brief post-lunch energizer. The energizer also served as a simulation of pressure situations, which they enjoyed, and the barrier was effectively broken. Subsequent processes that we preferred to carry out with desks out of the way were accepted without quibble by the supervisors.

On an earlier course for foremen (and they *were* all men) in an aerospace plant, we were accommodated in a much plusher room (the boardroom), with expensively upholstered chairs and no desks. It was almost impossible for the men to feel at home or protected in this environment. They had been sent on the course by senior managers with whom they enjoyed a chequered relationship. They were already suspicious and the surroundings didn't help. Not surprisingly the atmosphere was initially hostile. Their first question – and it wasn't meant as a joke – was 'Where are the microphones hidden?'. We learnt enough from this experience to subsequently leave the desks in place at the motor company – even though we generally preferred to start our workshops with a horseshoe or circular format.

Each of these dimensions, when handled well, creates attitudes that prepare trainees to experience the acceleration of inspirational training.

BREAKING THE ICE – WITH INSPIRATIONAL WARMTH

In groups of, say, 20 or fewer, with events lasting more than half a day, it is worth learning everyone's name. You can either do so privately, or perhaps use a name-learning game as an ice-breaker, so that everyone can benefit.

Here's a detailed sequence that:

- breaks the ice at the start of a course;
- introduces everyone;
- enables names to be remembered while teaching a useful basic memory technique;
- allows people to reveal more if they are happy to do so, without threatening those who do not.

ACTIVITY

Start by asking if it would be a valuable skill to be able to remember the names of people from the first time we meet them. While some participants say they don't bother making an effort because they assume they'll never meet again, most appreciate the potential advantages. Even for one-off encounters, you can make more of an impact by using the other person's name at some point during the proceedings.

Allocate a letter to each participant in turn – A, B, C and so forth. Then – beginning this time with a different person – give everyone a number – 1, 2, 3 and so on. Now everyone, including yourself, has a new 'name', such as A4, B7, C5, G15. Make a few random checks to make sure everyone has the idea of the new name format and can remember their own.

Allow one or two minutes (one minute is enough for a group of 10) for people to mix. In that time they are to introduce themselves to as many people as possible with their new names, and remember as many as they can.

Ask for volunteers to recall the names of three or more people, pointing to the person as they name them. Each person called should acknowledge whether or not they've been called by the right name: 'Yes, I'm B9'.

continued on page 35

The chances are that hardly anyone remembers three names. For someone to remember five is exceptional. Generally, the ones best remembered (if you have them) are K2 or A4, which can be associated with Himalayan mountains and English roads respectively. We can point out that while some things (mountains and roads, for example) are named by use of this format, they are clearly not easy to remember, and that the easiest way in which the memory is able to fix them is by some sort of association.

Visual associations are a powerful way for many people to remember things. And the next round of the exercise trades on visual clues.

ACTIVITY

Invite each participant to invent a name for themselves, applying the formula of an adjective followed by a noun. Each person then announces their name to the group, so that you can check everyone has understood.

continued on page 36

The sort of names which people select might be 'Green Mountain', 'Young Fish' or 'Rusty Nail'. My favourite was 'Average Golfer'.

Here you are encouraging participants to start improvising. Instead of being given a name, they are making one up for themselves. In addition, the exercise has the formula of freedom within structure that is characteristic of improvisation. The structure is simple and containing – the requirements are satisfied by any adjective followed by any noun. Even so, some people find it hard to deal with this degree of freedom, and ask for help in choosing a name for themselves.

You can reduce the pressure by reassuring hesitant participants that they won't be stuck with the name for more than a few minutes. The best way to help is to appreciate that the difficulty is generally one of commitment. People can think of names but are worried about revealing something damaging, or of what others might think – that the name 'isn't good enough', is 'too clever' or 'too unlikely'. If you anticipate this stumbling-block, you can mention a few example combinations at the start, then announce something pleasingly extreme to give licence to everyone's imagination. 'My name is Unmade Bed.'

Suggest that any name will do – however mundane or wild. It is a characteristic of improvisation that content is disposable. In this instance, for example, we only need the content for the length of the recall activity.

35

A weaker way to help if someone has difficulty in choosing a name is to allow suggestions from other participants. While it may be necessary eventually to permit this in order to keep the exercise moving, wait awhile, because it is far more empowering for people to think up and commit themselves to their own name.

Whilst the names chosen here are temporary, the experience of empowerment can be longer-lasting. For the moment we are simply practising our powers of invention – it happens to be names we are making up. Soon, though, we shall acknowledge the importance of real, lasting names, and raise the issue of more significant choice.

ACTIVITY

When everyone has a name, ask the group to mix again for one or two minutes, introducing themselves by their new names.

Ask volunteers to name as many new names as possible.

continued below

This time, when we ask for volunteers to recall as many names as possible by pointing to the people named, the results tend to be more impressive. It is quite easy for most people to remember three to five names, and there are regularly a few people in a group of 12 who can recall all or all but one.

One of the participants or the trainer can state that the images prompted by the names allow the mind to link together the person, the image and the (words of the) name. We see the person, which triggers the image and reminds us of the name.

The pace and style of the sequence now change again, as everyone finds a comfortable space (sitting in a circle usually works well).

ACTIVITY

Ask all participants in turn to state their real name and say what they feel or think about it.

continued on page 37

The option to express feeling or thoughts is to keep men and women comfortable. There is a theory that women prefer to say (or be asked) what they feel, and men what they think. The responses given in this part of the exercise give us an incidental chance to test the theory. The main point, however, is to give all participants an opportunity to reveal their reaction to their own name – perhaps even tell a story. Often, for example, a person known generally by an abbreviation of their name – say, Jon for Jonathan, Sam for Samantha – will recall a dislike of the full version, because that was what he or she was called whenever in trouble with his or her parents.

Most of us use the names that we were given. Others have chosen to change them for one reason or another. Many women change surname when they get married, for example.

The stories and reactions remind participants of the importance of calling people by the name they prefer.

ACTIVITY

Ask all participants in turn what they want you to call them today.

continued on page 39

Sometimes people enjoy adopting a new name for the session or even for forever after. As well as offering an opportunity for reflection, the exercise reinforces the point that people feel that their name matters. Several individuals may be feeling this most powerfully right now, having never considered this deeply personal, but easily accessible, matter before and having expressed it succinctly and safely to a room full of strangers or business colleagues. It is an elegant exercise, which retains its interest in groups of up to 40 people, whether they are strangers or colleagues. The real-name section can, of course, be detached from the memory-based parts of the sequence.

Not every exercise is appropriate for every programme. The inspirational trainer brings a boxful of tools and makes a final selection as the work progresses. The choice of whether or not to include the real-name discussion, for example, can be left until you have a feel for the group.

To run this particular part of the process, the trainer must be prepared to deal with whatever emotions arise in the group. Some people become sad or angry when telling their name stories. It is essential to allow the emotion to be expressed and to acknowledge each person's story with a 'thank you'. We do not have to try to make things right by offering comment, comfort or advice.

On your feet

Get all the participants back on to their feet, and out of deep contemplation, with the final part of the memory sequence. Explain that we filter information into our brains through three main channels – sight, sound and touch. Our other senses, taste and smell, are less often involved in most training contexts. If it is a culinary or wine-tasting course, then we can adapt accordingly. Smell is perhaps particularly underused. Consider, for example, how the smell of your old school brings back all manner of memories.

In Neuro-Linguistic Programming (NLP) literature you will find the three main channels called respectively visual, auditory and kinaesthetic. Kinaesthetics encompass touch, movement and their associated feelings. Some say that we each have a preferred channel for taking in information: some like to see things, some to hear them, others to learn by touching and moving. Noticing how you typically express yourself may indicate your own preferred channels. Visual learners, it is suggested, talk about 'getting the picture, seeing what you say, keeping an eye on things'. Auditory people 'hear the message', find that 'it rings a bell' and 'sounds good to them'. Kinaesthetics tend to 'stay in touch', 'get a handle on it' and say that 'it feels right to them'.

This is a simplified version of the theory and is worth proposing for the impact it can make during a training exercise. The fuller reality is that we process sensory information in complex ways, using different senses in a variety of ways in different circumstances.

I would offer this much theory to any group: beyond that, it depends. Scientists and engineers, in my experience, thrive on theory and love to know how these processes work and why they are doing them. They enjoy hearing about the latest brain research and appreciate explanatory diagrams in their participants' packs. Others, including entrepreneurs, are content to test the techniques and use them if they work.

While a learner may prefer one representational system, each of us is generally able to take in information through all the channels and develop every capability.

For the trainer, the important point is to deliver messages that cover all the systems. That way everyone is more likely to be reached. Later, we may benefit by finding out more about individuals' preferred ways of learning and adapt our materials to appeal more effectively to them. In one-to-one coaching, this is an important skill.

The Names game combines all three systems into one exercise. If people discover one element is the key to their memory, they will be able to adapt the technique for themselves, concentrating on just that channel.

┌─── ACTIVITY ───┐

Explain that participants are going to use sound, vision and movement to give their brains every chance of remembering each other's names.

Ask the participants to think of an active word which starts with the same sound as their name, and for which they can do a simple mime.

Demonstrate. Say, 'I'm Punching Paul', as you perform a punching mime with your hands.

Ask everyone to repeat the mime, while saying 'Punching Paul' and looking at you.

Go round the circle in turn, hearing the person's chosen name and alliterative description, then copying their activity.

As before, volunteers attempt to recall as many names as possible. The first couple of volunteers use the full description with the action. Then point out that it's unusual to say 'Hello Jumping Jack' while leaping into the air at the moment of greeting and ask for just the name. Continue to allow the hint of the appropriate movement, so that the kinaesthetic learners have that channel still available to them.

└──┘

This way, people can test their preferred learning channel for themselves by discovering whether they find it easier to recall the name by using only the movement, only the image or only the sound. Some realize their preferences quickly. For others the mental sequence is so fast that the names are memorized before they can identify which was the most effective part of the process. No matter, they can use the full technique easily next time they wish to remember a name.

Name-calling and mistakes

Years later, people meet and recall Dancing Denise or Freezing Frank. Avoid making comments on the psychology of the chosen epithets. When introduced to Depressing Dave, Suicide Sam and Naughty Nikki, simply let it pass.

Sometimes someone says that people rarely introduce themselves as 'Leaping Larry'. Acknowledge their observation, and suggest that when they meet someone they make up their own associational epithet and movement. The more vivid the image, the easier it is to remember, so we can use whatever appeals to us. Just be careful not to reveal it as you introduce people to each other in delicate social situations.

As you would with any practical exercise with an obvious application in the outside world, invite the participants to adopt it for their action plan. Encourage them to practise the technique at their next meeting or interview when they will benefit from remembering names.

When the student has trouble remembering the name of one new individual, their plan should be aimed at their next single introduction, before they ambitiously apply the technique to a roomful of 30 people.

Items fade from our memory unless we use them. Tony Buzan (1974: 63) reports that 80 per cent of facts are forgotten the day after we hear them unless we review the information. With names, it is socially acceptable and helps the memory to repeat them after we are told them. Then we should continue to use them to minimize the chance of memory fading. I have noticed that although some trainees have grasped the technique and their memories are in good working order, they continue to be poor with names, because they lack the confidence to use the system in real life. It helps them develop confidence in the technique and in themselves if you create an atmosphere during the training programme in which it won't matter if they get names wrong. Instruct everyone to use names whenever appropriate, and obtain agreement that no one will mind if people get their names wrong while they are practising. When a group agrees to permit mistakes, it is well on the way to enjoying the benefits of inspirational training.

You could set up a system on a programme whereby everyone tries to meet a quota of, say, two mistakes in each session. This not only counters the perfectionist tendencies that prevent some participants attempting things they perceive as risky, it also encourages new behaviours and validates mistakes in advance. Allowing mistakes sets the scene for further improvisation and opens the way for creative risk-taking. Getting a name wrong counts as a good mistake, because it indicates that the trainee is trying things out in an important and potentially painful territory.

You can apply the associative technique to any memory need. I suggest using it for names, because these are so fundamental, and provide trainees with a useful confidence-building resource that they can employ with immediate advantage.

Another simple and effective way to handle the question of names, especially if any of the course outcomes refer to creativity (or anything remotely like it), is to ask participants to make their own name badges, using felt tips, coloured pens and interesting papers. I have used this for a group of 200 participants, actively involving them all from the start. It also meant less work for the trainers – we simply supplied the materials and the trainees did the rest. Encourage people to use each other's names whenever they can. It is an effective way to connect.

Similarly, name-based tasks can be set to reflect course content. We invited people to make comedy badges when they joined a night-class for stand-up comedy. At another event I was invited to make my own name-plate, to lead to consideration of design. Later in the day, we were asked to improve the name-plate. It was a neat way of considering possibilities of greater elegance, visibility and panache.

THE SCENE IS SET

From joining instructions to simple ways of enhancing the environment, you can create conditions in which learning will flourish. Right from the outset, use music, fresh air and names to re-assure and involve participants, while stretching your creative talents too.

NSPIRATIONS

- Write joining instructions to create a sense of anticipation.
- Select a venue that has inspirational qualities of its own. Then enhance that environment with a rich array of learning materials.
- Check the acoustics and use music to create an atmosphere.
- Select a layout that suits the style of the session.
- Break the ice and learn names with an engaging activity.
- Allow your participants to be creative and make choices – their inspiration matters most.

Bonding

Bonding is the process by which the participants form into a cohesive group; it is facilitated by certain types of ice-breaker and techniques for keeping trainees directed towards the tasks and subjects of the programme.

Win participants' confidence by putting your stamp on proceedings from the outset. Like a party host, you can then lead or step into the background whenever needed. Your well-planned structure gives you the flexibility for freedom. Room preparations and greetings have set the scene for easing into the programme. Your next steps are probably a mix of:

- showing the big picture;
- dealing with immediate concerns and distractions;
- considering objectives;
- turning individuals into a group;
- establishing the rules of the programme.

While all these aspects need to be tackled reasonably early, the order in which to take them can vary according to the group and programme. You could deliberately fail to deal with distractions at the start of a time management course, for example, waiting until a distraction prompts a session about distractions. Conversely, you could respond to an unusually distracted group by finding out straight away what was bothering them. I remember a regular group which was failing to bond at the start of one session because most of them were listening for a helicopter to land in the field next to us for another event later in the day.

THE BIG PICTURE

Some people like to have an overview of what they will be encountering during a programme. If they are given this at the beginning, they will feel comfortable about subsequent details. Others are quite happy to dive straight into the components of the course, and find out later how these details fit the overall pattern. Nevertheless, it remains advisable to show the big picture first because, while a short session about the programme as a whole will not upset the latter group, the former would be lost without it.

Because people prefer to access their information in different ways, it is best to present summaries of the course in the form of:

- a big picture – visually, using photos, diagrams or icons;
- written information – by writing headings under the pictures;
- a timetable – or at least a list of events in their likely sequence;
- a 'route map' – when appropriate, perhaps instead of the big picture, or for a change at the beginning of a second or subsequent day;
- a spoken introduction – for those who prefer to hear what is going to happen.

It may seem repetitive for the trainer to convey the same information a number of times, but it is the variety of forms of communication that is important. You present in parallel rather than sequence, so it needn't take long. You deliver the introduction verbally, making reference to the big picture that is unveiled on the wall, ready captioned, and to the timetable which the participants have to hand inside the course pack. In this way you cover everybody's need to know enough to be comfortable as they set out on the programme.

DEALING WITH CONCERNS AND DISTRACTIONS

Other essential information that the participants need early includes:

- the whereabouts of toilets;
- entitlement to leave the room or building;
- the intention to take frequent breaks.

Once these are covered, you still need to deal with participants' concerns about the programme or about aspects of their lives which are nothing to do with the forthcoming event but which will prevent them from gaining the maximum benefit from it. Both areas, if neglected, are blocks to learning and need to be allayed so that they do not derail your plans for productive sessions.

One way to diminish a concern is simply to air and share it. Offer everyone this opportunity if they are attending a complex course, likely to engender concerns in each participant; or allow a minute or so for anyone to state what's on his or her mind.

Getting your message across

Figure 3.1 *A big picture*

I regularly teach courses in writing skills and know from experience that almost all the potential writers will be experiencing a particular set of fears, common to every writer I have met or heard about. However, I have adopted the tactic of waiting until the second session (one week after the first) to air and tackle these fears. An immediate advantage is that we don't take up a huge section of week one, when much else is taking place, so that the course can begin on a note of excitement rather than difficulty. By week two, the worries centre on their efforts at writing between the sessions. Other phantoms of concern will have disappeared of their own accord by this stage, and we can deal with those that really make a difference.

This tactic works with any regular course in which you feel confident that trainees' concerns will quickly disappear – or become more directed – as they grapple with the materials. There seems little purpose in encouraging fears or worries where none need exist, so provide scope for genuine concern, without forcing the issue.

An expressed concern may need only a simple acknowledgement – 'I note your concern' – or can be answered immediately: 'Yes it's fine to leave half an hour early to pick up your child'; 'No, you do not need your own calculator'. Some merit an immediate brief discussion – 'Shall we order a take-away lunch now?'. Others can be met with a promise that they are explicitly addressed later in the programme: 'Yes, we shall be covering bee-stings and snake-bites' (this is of course an example from a health and safety course, not customer care).

The deposit bank

An elegant method of dealing with the concerns of a large group without taking up much time is to establish the deposit bank.

__ ACTIVITY _____

Deposit bank
After handing out slips of paper or 'Post-Its' (about five per person is usually ample), ask the participants to write down any concerns or distractions which they have brought with them into the session.

Announce that they will soon be putting them aside by posting them into the deposit bank where they can collect them after the session if they wish. While in the bank, they will be forgotten. Then say, 'Now we have dealt with distractions, let's all switch off any machinery that is going to bleep', and build a pyramid of pagers and mobile phones.

At the end of the session, invite people to collect their worries from the bank (which can be a box, a board, or a table – the precise form doesn't matter), and to notice whether the deposit idea worked, and whether their worries have increased ('gathered interest') or diminished through being set aside.

This technique works as if by magic for most of those who use it. It's especially effective for concerns that have little to do with the course – that is those which it is possible to temporarily put aside and pick up again later, such as 'Will someone remember to feed the cat?' or 'Share prices could plummet again'. It also caters well for work worries that are left behind at the office/base while we are at the training event.

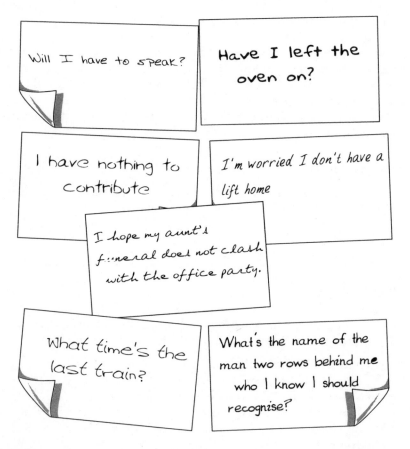

Figure 3.2 *The deposit bank of concerns*

The danger with this exercise is that it may encourage people to find worries where there are none. So, if the mood is clearly cheerful and positive as the session starts, give the deposit bank a miss. As ever in inspirational training, you have many options, a plan and flexibility.

If you do open a bank, tell the participants whether or not you will be reading their notes. They can provide useful insights into what is troubling your clientele. The issues may be easily addressed – if, for example, they are about logistics or timing – or they may be things that must be dealt with during the course or in some other format.

Case file
Deposit bearing interest
If we already know that there are many worries hovering over an event, we can provide more help in directing, articulating and dealing with them.

A one-day seminar with senior managers from two financial institutions that were merging resembled two gangs meeting on the neutral turf of a hotel halfway between their two cities. Everyone knew someone from the other group, but most people had yet to meet most of their counterparts.

There was a lot of new information to be conveyed, but it was clear that participants were unlikely to absorb much if they were worried about their individual futures after the merger. So we used a variant of the deposit bank – an appropriate concept for workers in that sector.

First we explained that we knew there were numerous concerns, and that these would be acknowledged and dealt with. Indeed, information presented during the day would answer many of their questions. We added that it was important they approach the day with an open mind.

Based on earlier discussions, we showed a slide with these categories and examples:

Distractions

- Have I fed the cat?
- Will I get a lift home?
- When's Uncle Ted going to get out of hospital?

Process concerns

- Will I be asked to speak?
- Will I be able to contribute usefully today?
- Are these guys from the other city human?

Content concerns

- Will I have to share a desk in the new office?
- What will my boss be like?
- Is this a merger or a takeover?

We asked everyone to write down anything that might prevent them from getting the best out of the event – whether they happened to be these or any others. We explained that it helps to give a name to our fears. By identifying what troubles us, we replace a vague cloud of worry with something we can confront and tackle – which in itself is often less frightening. Articulating a fear also often reveals seeds of a solution.

As the bank delegates walked to the edges of the room to stick their stickers on the boards, we asked them to form groups of three, containing at least one representative from each of the two offices. This led them actively into their next process, so that they were unable to dwell on the dispatched concerns.

The event ran smoothly, and we were able to pick up and highlight a number of details from the boards, which proved helpful for designing further events in the merger process.

OBJECTIVES

Objectives can be clear, defined statements of minimum targets. Or they can be more ambitious and vague, where the satisfaction test is a feeling rather than an observable or measurable result. For example, the objective of 'better communication between the managers' could either be made more precise by adding specific criteria, or left vague on the assumption that the managers would readily recognize that communications had improved.

A programme probably starts with objectives already stated – perhaps in a letter sent in advance. Even so, they should be restated near the beginning, so that they are fresh in participants' minds. This also provides an opportunity for trainees to make objectives their own.

For example, within broad programme objectives of 'better public speaking and improved platform skills', we can ask each trainee to think of a forthcoming occasion on which it will benefit them to speak well. They are to imagine themselves doing so (forming a clear mental picture which will help guide them towards the goal and to recognize the moment when they have achieved it) and then write down the objective in their own words.

We can also ask participants to note what evidence would show they had achieved their objectives. When there is time, I ask them to share their objectives and criteria with the group. People are often amazed and reassured by how much they have in common, and find it illuminating to hear the differences in criteria expressed; this is particularly helpful for those whose goals are sometimes vague and who therefore benefit from sharpening their evidence criteria.

Managing expectations

The inspirational trainer enjoys hearing individuals' objectives. Listening attunes you and prepares you to deliver accurately. Trainees enjoy it too, as validation. You can even tap into one of the pleasures of modern consumers – shopping lists – as a way of making objectives more precise and courses more responsive.

Ask 'What do you want from the programme?' and list the answers. As well as honing objectives, this helps deals with expectations. Trainers need to manage expectations. If the course is not designed to supply the items which participants call out, we can make the advertised limitations clear. If we know we can go beyond their suggestions, we can immediately raise expectations by asking whether the trainees would like more.

Shopping list
These were the items on the shopping list for a four-session course of scriptwriting skills:

- Write some dialogue.
- Create realistic characters.
- Get started.
- Know which format is right for my ideas.
- Learn discipline.
- Find out how to structure a script.
- Complete a piece of writing.

This struck me as a list that showed under-expectation. Most of the items would be demonstrably achieved by the end of the second session. All would have been discussed and actioned by week three. I asked if the participants wanted to add further items, to do with writing structured scenes, integrating subplots, skilled handling of entrances/exits, scene starts and finishes, and finding one's own voice as a writer. These were all planned anyway as part of the sessions, were to an extent within the capacity of the writers, and enabled them to lift their expectations beyond their original ambitions.

Using a shopping list is an effective way to give participants a feeling of control over the programme. Such a sense of control is important, forming a secure base for learning. There is always a tension between the elements that participants feel they have under control and those which seem new or adventurous. The more we can help place items on to the 'under control' side, the more we can achieve with the unknown. We can move course contents across that line through negotiation. The list is something they negotiate for themselves with the trainer. In all probability, you'll find virtually the same shopping list appearing time after time. Yet the feeling of empowerment remains, and there is always the chance that something which the trainees want might persuade the trainer to adapt the session now or the next time around.

On a flexible course that is going well, one of the most useful questions to ask is 'What more do we need to do for you to meet your objectives?' This enlists trainees to devise and manage the rest of the programme with you in exactly the ways needed for all objectives to be met or surpassed.

BONDING GAMES

For most programmes, it helps if participants are happy to work with each other – whether that means supporting each individual in their distinctive aims or toiling collectively towards common purposes.

Often individuals arrive feeling frosty towards the other participants. Perhaps they are work colleagues with a history of antipathy. Maybe they feel fear or trepidation about the course. Many people worry about how they will appear to others on unfamiliar territory or performing novel feats. An insensitive approach can engender the feeling that we are all strangers.

So it is part of the trainer's job to help people feel at ease with each other. The traditional assumption is that the atmosphere is likely to be cool and that it should be warmed up with ice-breakers – processes aimed at getting participants to know each other better or work together more cooperatively. These are obviously deployed near the beginning of a programme, and sometimes also at the start of subsequent sessions.

My view is that the better processes used as ice-breakers contain hidden riches which could be mined at any point in the timetable. Which to use when depends on their key features. As you would expect, many traditional ice-breakers are bonding games, but others are perfect gateways into all sorts of routes – the Name game in the previous chapter, for example, contains material for enhancing memory and making choices. In some ways, ice-breaking processes are at the heart of improvisational learning, epitomizing active, participatory modes.

By sequencing the examples I describe and harnessing the concepts that underlie them in order to create your own training processes, you will be equipped to customize every programme.

The sophisticated trainer finds or devises an ice-breaker that is integral to the course. On my Confidence and Creativity open programme, for example, where participants are unlikely ever to see each other again, and it is not their concern how everyone else fares, it would be disconcerting if they faced ice-breakers which seemed to be primarily about group bonding. We do need some cohesion for the day to succeed, and everyone can appreciate that, but we use ice-breakers which operate on a more individual level. Sometimes this is only a matter of phrasing – of how processes are presented. It's the difference between 'We're going to work as a group' and 'You will each individually be aware of how comfortably you can function within a group'.

Where individuals have a greater investment in each other's progress – in teambuilding events, for example – make the bonding process more explicit in introductions and debriefings.

Rituals

A group can bond through rituals – shared proceedings which acquire added meaning through familiarity and a sense of exclusivity. Build ritual into programmes overtly or covertly. Covert ritual may be as simple as starting each day with the same format – a horseshoe setting, perhaps, with each participant invited in turn to state in a sentence or two how they are feeling.

More overt rituals include lighting a candle before the start of each session. I have seen this used most effectively to entice strangers into becoming a reasonably cohesive group prepared to undertake some drama exercises together. The trainer told us it was to remind us of the sacred origins of drama, and the candle would remain alight throughout the session.

The trainer John Delves began a day of lecturing to 100 or so managers by saying that he was familiar with our famous British reserve, but wanted everyone to shout 'Good morning' when he said 'Good morning'. After three goes he was satisfied with the quality of the collective shout and asked for a similar volume and response when he greeted the group at each session. This duly occurred, until he 'forgot' to say 'good afternoon' after the tea break, at which point several members of the audience reminded him to do so, because by now they wanted their ritual shout.

Elements of ritual build participants' confidence by creating a feeling of belonging. We tend to feel more confident when other people share our actions and beliefs. When the action is distinctive, the sharing is more apparent. Tribes often make their rituals painful in order to increase the feelings of common experience and of crossing psychological lines. Once someone pays a significant price to go through a barrier, they tend to value their membership more.

Ritual can be seen as a long-term strategy for creating motivation: if you are irrevocably part of the tribe, you are more likely to subscribe to its aims. The sinister example of this process is, of course, the humiliating and painful rituals used by gangs to create passivity in their members. You can rest assured that your rituals are on the positive and empowering side if they cause no pain or embarrassment, and if they are readily adopted by your training group on subsequent meetings even without your prompting.

The security of being an accepted part of a group stands alongside the feeling of individual input and control as a base for improvisational learning.

Selecting a starter

It is certainly a good idea to select an ice-breaker which respects the participants' starting point. If they are likely to resist group-forming, then ice-breakers which begin with the assumption of groups are going to be more challenging for the trainer to implement and it will be easier to start with a process which involves them as individuals, such as Invisible Rules below, or the Photograph Introductions described in Chapter 9.

Working in pairs is one way of reducing the feeling of isolation which many people experience at the beginning of any course while still allowing them a sense of protection from full immediate exposure to the larger group. The processes in which trainees pair up and then introduce each other to a group break barriers gently.

RULES

If you are going to be with participants for three days or more, it is worth taking time to establish rules. You might want sessions to start promptly, for example, or for comments to be constructive rather than critical, or for personal abuse to be off-limits. Your clients may disagree, or request rules in dimensions you haven't considered. I worked with one group of local government officers whose only demand about confidentiality was that none of them should leak anything to their somewhat feared chief executive. This in itself told me much about the organization.

Part of the trainer's inspirational bargain is to allow trainees as much leeway as possible, and rules which a group chooses for itself are the most likely to be kept. While most procedural rules can be established without problems, there are deeper rules that a trainer can bring to the surface. A sequence such as Invisible Rules is appropriate for programmes dealing with creativity, personal or organizational change, or any session in which you want to:

- energize the opening session;
- provoke a great deal of thought;
- warm everyone physically and mentally;
- engender profound insights;
- lead into a consideration of rules.

Invisible rules

ACTIVITY

Rules

Ask everyone to go around the room individually, at the same time, pointing to any object that catches their eye and naming the object out loud.

continued on page 54

I describe this as a mental warm-up, and instil a sense of urgency and motivation by asking people to name as many different objects as possible in one minute. You'll find a heightening of alertness, as people notice the extraordinary number of objects in even the dullest training room.

Sometimes participants experience some disquiet, usually because they are operating individually and aren't sure if they're getting it right or wrong. With improvisational activities we try to break away from the rigidities of right and wrong. The game is simply played. Knowledge may derive from experience, but in this case it won't be knowledge about 'correctness'.

> ─── **ACTIVITY** ──────────────────────────
>
> Now ask the participants to spend one minute, again simultaneously, pointing to things in the room, whilst naming aloud the object they were previously pointing at.
>
> *continued below*

If they haven't tried this before – and the chances are that most haven't – it is quite tricky, but also reasonably swiftly mastered. So there is generally a sense of achievement, and also laughter as frustration and tension are released.

> ─── **ACTIVITY** ──────────────────────────
>
> Third, we go free-form. Again, give the group one minute in which to point at things and name them out loud, only this time ask them to give whatever name they wish to each object they point at. Say, 'Point at things and name them whatever you want.'
>
> *continued below*

In theory, this should be tremendously liberating. There are patently no rights or wrongs, you are doing it on your own and nobody is judging you anyway. Yet, typically, participants find this part of the exercise much harder than the brain-teasing second section. Freedom alone fails to result in flow.

> ─── **ACTIVITY** ──────────────────────────
>
> Ask the participants why they find the third part of the exercise difficult. Collect the answers.
>
> *continued on page 55*

Often people do not know why they find the free-form part of the exercise difficult. I contend that they are working in the region of their blind spots – encountering the invisible workings of ideology. And the intriguing nature of the paradox – that this should be very easy, but strangely turns out to be difficult – encourages an investigation into this shadowy area.

Collecting the answers, which often include 'embarrassment', 'couldn't think of anything', 'I wanted to call everything by a different name from everything else, but got stuck in a category', allows us to reframe the answers in the form of rules.

┌─── **ACTIVITY** ─────────────────────────────────────┐

Get the group into a circle and elicit the rules which people were
following. The quickest way is for people to call them out as they
identify them.

continued below

The rules tend to include:

- Don't call anything by its real name.
- Don't use the same name more than once.
- Don't copy what anyone else says.
- Don't say anything that could be taken as offensive (however mildly)
  by anyone who happens to overhear.
- If I find that I'm naming things from a single category (a fruit shop or
  zoo, for example) then I should change category as quickly as possible.

All of these rules – and others, which may or may not have been in play,
and may or may not have been identified – were self-imposed. None of
them was a rule of the game as given.

For many participants, this is a moment of insight, revelation or relief.
For some, the insight is followed quickly by a veil of worry – where else
am I applying such unnecessary constraints? This is because it is apparent
to them that if they are restricting themselves without realizing it in a simple
game, they may well be restricting themselves with far more significant
consequences elsewhere in their lives. As James P Carse (1986) writes: 'What
will undo any boundary is the awareness that it is our vision, and not what
we are viewing, that is limited'. Each of the self-imposed rules makes the
game harder to play, by constraining the options, increasing fear and worry
and destroying flow. (I am assuming here that a feeling of ease and a sense
of flow are desirable outcomes. Although no particular outcome is specified
by the rules, participants do wonder why they have yet to experience the
ease and flow they expect.) In combination, assumed rules can make even
the most willing and imaginative participants dry up rapidly.

Rules establish a range of limitations. They restrict freedom of manoeuvre,
though often allowing considerable room for choice within their restraints.

┌─── **ACTIVITY** ─────────────────────────────────────┐

Take each rule in turn, question whether or not it is desirable to apply
it, and then play the game again, having abandoned the unwanted
'rules'. The game will flow much better the second time round.

Often the next question is 'where did those rules come from?'. You may or may not want to explore this issue, depending on whether the learning points available are relevant to the training course objectives.

Here are some suggestions of what prompts the rules, which offer an indication of how they might lead into later sessions about instructions, efficiency, communications or creativity (for example):

- **Don't call anything by its real name.**
  Well, that would be too easy. The assumed challenge of the game is to think up a word different from the word that springs to mind when we look at an object (which tends to be its usual name).

  Most people are suspicious of anything that seems too easy. Even children, if given a simple instruction, tend to impose complications. We don't usually take instructions on-board unless the task is going to be difficult – that is, worth instructing. If we can do it anyway, why bother with instructions? The answer is that instructions are important for all sorts of reasons. There may be a sequence to be learnt, for example, in which each individual step is simple, but the point is to get the order correct. Or, as in this game, once you accept that it is all right for an activity to be easy, you gain benefits. If you reject such ease, the game is harder. Unless there are strong reasons otherwise, learners gratefully accept what is easy and obvious.

- **Don't use the same name more than once.**
  Again, the assumption concerns implicit challenge. If you have done the thinking to generate the word, and have used that word, then the word and the thinking behind it is used up and it is incumbent on you to devise a new one. This strand of thinking does not usually trouble anyone who understands the rationale of mass-production, printing presses, systems of royalties or repeat fees. There's no overriding reason why we shouldn't enjoy multiple benefits from one piece of effort. For seminars about marketing, this opens the door to consideration of franchises and syndication.

- **Don't say anything that could be taken as offensive (however mildly) by anyone who happens to overhear what I say.**
  Here the self-imposed rule is social, guarding against embarrassment or giving offence. It is also the reason why most people play the game quietly – especially during an ice-breaking session. The privacy of near-silence is a powerful shield.

  Sometimes it is liberating for a group to lift this rule and deliberately operate against it, shouting random rude things at each other: this can lead to exploration of areas such as trust, aggression, sensitivity and so on. With a reserved group of British managers, this might be better saved for a final-night after-dinner occasion.

Some groups choose to keep a rule about not offending others, or censoring themselves to avoid rude words. And that's fine – it is a social rule, freely chosen, and does not slow the game down much.

- **Don't copy what anyone else says *and* if I'm naming things all from one category (fruit shop or zoo, for example) then I should change category as quickly as possible.**

Why do we impose it on ourselves to not copy, not repeat, not stay in one category? If we turn the rules around, they seem to be saying 'be original' and 'be creative' which are, of course, 'Good Things'. Yet these rules also seem to be defining originality and creativity in an extremely limiting fashion. Originality, defined in terms of not doing something – for example, not allowing yourself to copy those around you – is constraining and pressurizing. As a result, little that is original actually emerges.

Paradoxically, the barrier against copying operates as a barrier to originality. Participants freeze and tend to confine themselves to naming the obvious, safest, most banal features of the room. Perhaps the rule is imposed because the action of copying reminds people of school, where similar copying was regarded as cheating. As being too easy.

Yet most advances are made by copying first, then going beyond. We see further by standing on another's shoulders. In the game, everyone is an individual, following their own route and making their own choices, but they are not isolated; they hear what others are saying, and are entitled to say the same, or to say something prompted in their mind by another. When this happens, as one idea sparks off another, there is more originality, and creativity seems to bounce around the room. A similar principle is at work in collective brainstorming. Why hear something said by another player, and work hard and negatively in order not to make anything of it?

Refusing to stay in one category is another interesting limitation. It displays an urgent desire to move on before making full use of where we are.

In improvised performances by actors, for example, they sometimes fail to explore fully the idea in the scene. Suddenly, they move on, leaving potential frustratingly untapped. The converse is to spend too long on one aspect, which is even more obvious and boring. Either way, the audience senses it, and feels oddly unsatisfied. What's missing is a sense of completeness: of having reached, recognized and acted on the moment to move on. In business, too, there is an important balance to be struck between fulfilling potential (of an idea or product) and stagnation.

When the game is over, ask the participants what rules they would like for their course. Another option – depending on the nature of the programme – is to allow them to explore any rules which they may be imposing on themselves and following unknowingly and damagingly in more complex settings. This is a valuable exercise, for example, near the start of a senior managers' strategy conference.

The Invisible Rules game provides the satisfying experience that follows dropping self-imposed rules. In this game, the benefits consist of feeling 'flow' and realizing that some surprising choices lead to greater success.

BASE CAMP IS SECURE

By playing these introductory elements in almost any order, isolated individuals will bond into a group, with shared, realistic expectations. Their concerns have been expressed, acknowledged and dealt with, they have contracted in to their own rules, started to take responsibility for their own learning and begun to form a cohesive unit by means of their own rituals.

The participants will already be learning the skills and pleasures of expressing themselves more openly, sharing information with others and dissolving mental blocks in order to free their imaginations. They will be doing this in a relatively unpressured way, keeping control for themselves, choosing the pace at which to engage and how much to reveal. Good ice-breakers leave everyone feeling that they have succeeded in the task and have gained something from doing so. As a result, both you and your trainees will be better equipped to appreciate the moment and attune yourselves to sense when it is time to move on.

NSPIRATIONS

- Begin with the big picture.
- Deal with concerns and distractions early.
- Find out what the participants want to achieve on the day, and how they will know they have done so.
- Use rituals to help the group to bond, allowing as much leeway as possible for them to set their own rules and create their own ways of doing things.

4

The trainer as model

What the trainer does is at least as important as what the trainer says. To improve participants' performance, bring all your own inspirational skills and qualities into sessions.

Whether you are engaged as a consultant or are already part of the organization, you are increasingly expected to operate as a model of the kind of confidence, creativity and improvisational abilities you encourage in your trainees.

If you are teaching communication, you need to be an expert communicator. If teaching presentation skills, you'll be expected to be a fine presenter. As the Americans say, you have to 'walk the talk'.

If we perform the skill we are trying to impart, we can be copied. Participants will respect us when we clearly know the subject and can demonstrate our own mastery of it. The reverse is true too: if we act contrarily to what we teach, we rapidly lose authority.

The archetypal trainer is a skilled practitioner of what's being taught. And the obvious conclusion is that the better the practitioner, the better the training will be. We go to a cordon bleu chef to learn cooking. Most football coaches were once top players. This is the seductive logic of the masterclass.

THE MASTERCLASS

In the context of inspirational training, the masterclass has a place in the repertoire. If you are yourself a master, you have a valuable edge. If you are not, don't despair. You can invite mastery into your class whenever you need. The main use of a masterclass – live or on video – is as a vivid, detailed and richly complete demonstration. It serves as an opportunity for modelling, as inspiration for best practice and as a springboard to help the aspirant find ways of making the leap to expert.

I remember Thelma Schoonmaker, film editor to the director Martin Scorsese, presenting a series of clips to a group of film students in South Wales, explaining how they made the sound effects. The noise of Robert de Niro hitting his boxing opponent on the head during *Raging Bull* was apparently created by chopping a cabbage. Thelma spent a short time with us and, after she had answered questions, we capitalized on the inspiration she had provided by returning to the cutting rooms to work on our own films.

I also remember a famous illustrator leading a class in drawing cartoons. One of his skills was drawing quickly – so quickly that there was little hope of picking up any technical points. His talent for explanation was so limited that he might better have simply delivered pictures for us to copy or admire.

This points to the fallacy of masterclass logic. The best player may not be the best teacher. Our wonderful chef may be a disastrous communicator. What makes them special may be precisely what prevents them from passing it on. A practitioner may benefit from being selfish, secretive, obsessed or not analytical. A trainer needs other qualities. The great actor Ian McKellen realized this: 'I know exactly what an actor wants – and I can't give it to him', he said (1991), explaining why he was not a director.

So, while the masterclass has its place, it is far from being the whole story. To succeed as a trainer, the master needs to be a good communicator and be able to bring expertise to bear by turning on the magic of perform-ance to order during a course.

Another problem is that expert practitioners do not always realize precisely what makes them so good. They may value one aspect of their craft, while their significant contribution could lie elsewhere. It may take an outside observer to notice this.

A better trainer will be the analyst who can identify the nature of excellence and articulate it in ways that can be understood by learners. This is the insight behind the NLP concept of modelling, which is a structured, experimental form of copying. For trainers, one use of this idea is to distrust what experts say they do and concentrate on what they actually do – and to notice what works.

Organizations don't need the best practitioners for their training; they need the best trainers. The trainer is probably going to be a 'good enough' practitioner.

There was great merit in the old classroom idea, originating with the Romans and practised in many societies since, in which pupils who were one or two years ahead were responsible for teaching the juniors. They knew more than them, but not too much more. Whatever they taught was unlikely to be way over the heads of the learners and it was probably current. It also helped that they still recalled what it was like to be at the lower level.

Many of these instructors would have patience because they themselves remembered being the learner, although perhaps the flaw in the system is that it demands a great degree of tolerance from the young leaders. It is difficult for many teachers and mature trainers to keep recalling what it was like not to know. A gentler version of the system, which preserves most of the advantages, is evident in current practices of mentoring.

Another approach, known as 'Action Learning', is for groups to learn with minimal expert support. A group may, for example, start a subject from scratch, or with only a modicum of outside tuition, and develop their own skills. Teams of circus performers, stand-up comedians and script-writers – as well as many managers – have worked successfully in this way. This seems a fruitful method where there is a high degree of self-motivation and little set curriculum.

STRENGTH IN LIMITS

Training can be arduous enough without excessive and unrealistic demands. The inspirational trainer appreciates that it is not necessary to be able to do everything. Nor is it necessary to know everything. It is wise to accept that participants will know more about their special areas of expertise than we do, and for us to admit this. Part of anybody's expertise is to recognize his or her own limits.

What, then, do trainers model? Is there a single prototype trainer to whom anyone can point, saying 'That's the good model'? No, because there are many excellent trainers and many excellent ways of training.

Nonetheless, there are certain qualities and practices which most good trainers have in common. Trainees can observe these and copy them, absorb them subconsciously, or simply respect them. Some of these qualities will be pertinent to the content of the programme. Others are more concerned with process – with how we teach rather than the formal subject.

As a trainer, you may or may not be a master of the subjects that you are offering. You will, however, be a model to your trainees, in at least some of the following areas.

The 14 key inspirational qualities

1. clear thinking;
2. empathy;
3. subject knowledge;
4. resourcefulness;
5. humility;
6. knowing how to find information;
7. intuition;
8. patience and tolerance;
9. good humour;
10. presentation skills;
11. flexibility;
12. facilitation skills;
13. confidence;
14. the ability to let go.

Clear thinking

In almost any training programme, clear thinking will be deemed a virtue. The trainer can demonstrate its value in everything from good planning to on-the-spot insights during each session.

Whether or not the issue of clear thinking needs to be made manifest depends on the programme. In a course of time management or efficiency procedures, a confident trainer might challenge the group to design a more efficient timetable for the programme itself and then make use of the best ideas.

You can give the appearance of clear thinking by taking plenty of time to plan your courses, including alternative routes to deal with 'What ifs?' Participants do not need to be aware of the efforts you have made to wrest the materials into logical order.

If you find it difficult to think clearly during a course when you are under pressure, create time for yourself – for example, by calling a break, or asking the group members to sort something out for themselves.

Empathy

To work well with a group, it helps if a trainer can judge the moods of individuals and of the group itself. This may be accomplished by observation – by simply looking for signs that the group members are engaged, alert body postures and quick and accurate responses to questions, discussion prompts and instructions. It may be done by listening. There is a technique of empathetic listening, for example, in which without judgement, you reflect back the emotion: 'You sound angry. . .'. Or you can keep track of mood by soliciting feedback. Ask your group to let you know when they feel it is time to speed up, slow down or take a break.

Empathy then takes this process a step further. After identifying the mood, the trainer takes it into account, first by accepting, then either by acknowledging, questioning or even challenging. Having empathy means you are attuned to another's wavelength, and it is a skill worth developing – mainly through listening, watching, and occasionally pausing during our own activities.

I have seen trainers completely misread a group and consequently lose trust. In one instance, key individuals were restless for some reason and challenged a fairly innocuous graph, designed to illustrate a connection between rewards and motivation. The trainer was uncertain how to defend the theory and began to flounder. If she had sensed the mood, she could easily have said, 'You may find this graph useful, or you may not. There are several other models and illustrations, which may prove more appropriate to your particular circumstances. Let's move on to something else'. This would have bought time, and with shifting the mood, the graph would probably have escaped further criticism. Alternatively, she could have taken the comments in a non-defensive spirit and agreed that the graph was weak.

One option in such circumstances is to request co-operation in finding something more illuminating. This is best done from a position of strength. If a trainer already feels or seems weak, then asking for help can be a dangerous tactic in that it transfers authority to the group and you may exercise insufficient credibility to bring it back again when needed. For a confident trainer, on the other hand, soliciting the group's help can be a winning tactic, particularly when the trainer understands the need for humility.

Sufficient subject knowledge

While you may not know everything about the subject, it helps to know something. Before a session, you can ask someone to brief you. Find out the three most important things about the topic. Discover the structure of the organization you are discussing. Knowing the broad outline allows you to fill in the detail as necessary as you go along.

What counts as sufficient depends on the process. You may be able to facilitate a game in groups without knowing anything about the main subject. You may know enough to lead a discussion, but would need to understand a deal more to give a lecture.

Humility

As a general rule, trainers should admit what they don't know. If you assess the weak areas of a programme in advance, then these admissions can be built into the design. If this is not possible, it is better to be frank about your shortcomings.

Case study

I was once asked to work with a construction firm on a project that had fallen behind schedule. Understandably, in the rush, there was insufficient time to arrange a full briefing before my series of workshops with the supervisory teams began, so we devoted one of the first sessions to analysing and describing the problems.

I said, 'I know very little about what's been happening on this project. You know every aspect, and I would appreciate it if you helped me understand'. The participants split into two groups to compile a prioritized list of reasons to explain why the work was lagging. Attending the course meant time away from their project, and they understandably wanted to know – and some of them asked aggressively – 'What can you do?'.

When I stressed the absence of prefigured solutions, they seemed pleased I wasn't claiming to have the answers, and certainly didn't mind my not knowing the details of a situation which they had been experiencing for many months.

In that atmosphere, we were able to begin to find levers implied by their analyses. The purpose of having two groups was to provide each group with a second perspective – to enjoy the advantages of stereo over mono.

By not knowing the details in advance, I was able to present myself as being more on their side than that of senior management, which led easily to solutions rather than blame.

Resourcefulness

Although at this point in the construction project I was working primarily on a process, I could contribute elements of content – in the form of tips and ideas – when I felt that the groups were missing something.

An inspirational trainer aims to be a model of resourcefulness – a repository of ideas that can be injected when needed or requested. Resourcefulness is to do with filling gaps, and an improvisational attitude helps you to spot opportunity. When a group of actors arrived to perform a comedy show one night and discovered they had no props, their solution was to ask the audience to contribute items. They then improvised with the donated props, impressing the audience more than if they had brought the planned items. The tactic was so successful that it became a regular feature of the show.

As well as sourcing and supplying materials, the trainer may be an information resource. If you already have background materials pertinent to the programme content, bring them along. An instant library of books, tapes and so on at the back of the room provides an extra dimension, permitting participants to browse during breaks, investigate other perspectives and obtain some idea of a subject's scope. A reading list to supplement the course notes adds to your authority and evident expertise.

However, on some programmes, you may not have sufficient budget, time or information to provide all the resources you might like. What is perhaps more important – and certainly serves as an excellent model – is to know how to find pertinent information.

Knowing how to find information

To find information, you need to combine the skills of a librarian and a journalist. The best way to fill gaps in your knowledge of a subject is to ask questions designed to elicit the information sought. This is the classic Socratic method for advancing knowledge.

While acknowledging that you may not always have the answers, you can encourage trainees to hone their information searches by framing and asking questions about any aspect of the subject matter. The course will immediately benefit from the creation of an inquisitive atmosphere in which it is all right not to know, better to try to find out, and where pertinent information can be gathered and put to use. You can set the tone by asking questions of participants, guests, suppliers and so on. If you are concerned that questions may disrupt a particular process, let the participants know that they will have their chance at the end.

To help trainees obtain precise answers, encourage them to practise the traditional journalistic questions: 'Who?', 'What?', 'Where?', 'Why?' and

'When?'. If they want more discursive replies, suggest that they use open formats, such as 'Tell me about. . .'.

If the information is not at hand, either in the materials you have brought or in the heads of yourself or your trainees, places for finding quality intelligence include libraries, professional associations, the Internet, colleagues and friends. If you don't know, ask someone who might. When I was a journalist, I was taught that it was always possible to ask one more question in any interview. Stretching to find and ask that final question frequently resulted in the best nugget of information or the most fascinating story. It is a habit that trainers-as-models can usefully borrow.

Intuition

Use your instincts. Bring them to consciousness by saying to yourself, 'I know what's needed here. What is the right thing to do next?'.

In some organizations, intuitive behaviour comes as a revelation. You can gently model using instincts by informing participants when you are doing so: 'My intuition tells me you need 15 minutes to make notes on the last process, to sort out for yourselves what you learnt and how you are going to use that learning back at base'.

Patience, tolerance and good humour

With a learning group, the trainer can easily be tempted to keep pace only with the fastest learners. Yet part of the training responsibility is to help the slowest. Concepts 'click' for different people at different times. Your programmes will be full of satisfying clicks, but they will not necessarily be simultaneous.

If someone doesn't understand something, it is safest to assume that it is because you have yet to explain it clearly enough. Assume there exist no learning difficulties – only teaching challenges.

Presentation skills

Yes, presenting proves nerve-wracking for most people. The trick is to use the butterflies to your advantage. The adrenaline is your fuel for the demands of being on the platform.

Good presentation implies to students that the content is valuable. The presentation not only compels their attention towards the material, but also serves as a model for the increasing number of presentations each participant is likely to give in modern organizations.

Ways of improving your presentation are detailed in the following chapter.

Flexibility

The ability to make changes when needed is an art that is admired and appreciated by trainees. Many training programmes have timetables that are too tight and rigid. What is the virtue in getting through all the material if the material is not getting through? If an extra few minutes or one more activity will make a section clear and memorable, it is better to add it at that moment than to move on to conform to a preordained schedule.

Similarly, if prepared materials provide too little challenge to your group, drop them. Find something else. Always take a list of spare activities and think through various paths that the group might follow. This helps put you into a flexible frame of mind, ready to respond to the group immediately.

Facilitation

Facilitation means making things easy. Trainers constantly make judgements about when to intervene and when to leave alone. If you suspect you err on one side of that divide, look out for opportunities to exercise the other aspect. For trainers who become too involved too quickly, it can be most illuminating to observe a group work something out for themselves.

On the other hand, a facilitator with too light a touch might find that a timely intervention saves a fruitless discussion or that a neat summary crystallizes a point.

Confidence

Confidence lies:

- in your own abilities and knowledge;
- in the trainees' abilities;
- in the knowledge that the programme will work out well.

One way of being confident is to stay within realms in which you know you can deliver. If you promise no more than you intend to give, you can be reasonably sure of achieving it. If you then give more, that will be a bonus. This restriction, however, does little to stretch you. In order to build confidence and inspire yourself, you need to keep stepping out of the safety zone.

Carrying your feelings of confidence from one occasion to another, quite possibly dissimilar, situation is a good way to begin. It is effective to carry the confidence from a successful situation to one that's more challenging.

If you succeeded in making a sale to a regular customer, use the impetus to win a new client with the next cold call.

Assume you are at least as confident as anyone else in the same situation. If you are about to give a presentation, for example, remember that, in general, most other presenters have felt exactly as you do at that moment. The vast majority survived.

Even if you doubt your own abilities, you can retain confidence in the ability of your trainees. Rely on them from time to time to move the programme through difficult moments. Many trainers and teachers find it difficult to be confident about their charges. If this is the case, it can help to enlist the support of those participants in whom you have the most confidence. You can test this early in proceedings in small ways. For example, when collecting thoughts from the group onto a flip-chart, you can often ask someone to scribe. Almost invariably they prove equal to what can be a complex task.

Case study

On one course, I happened to know that one participant knew a great deal about assessments. I asked him privately if he had anything to add to the list of assessment methods I was about to show. He said the list was fine, and wondered if he had been saying too much in the group discussions. On the contrary, I assured him he had not been, and that anything he could contribute to the assessment session – where I was aware of his expertise – would be most appreciated. He then thoroughly enjoyed filling in any gaps that I left, and enhanced the process considerably.

Even if some sections of a course fail to match your expectations, it does not mean the whole programme is a disaster. Stay confident that the course will work as a complete entity. People will get from it what they need.

Any programme will gather its own momentum and, after a while, the trainer's task becomes gentle steering rather than brute pushing.

The ability to let go

Letting go means that the trainer does not have to win every argument, cap every discussion, or make sure everyone is involved in every exercise – let alone constantly enjoying it.

While facilitating is akin to hosting a party, it is for each participant to decide whether to take advantage of what's on offer and how best to do so. As you train inspirationally, you will note that learners often make surprising choices. Trainers gain respect by allowing things to happen in ways they haven't predicted and might not themselves have chosen. They can also give credit when participants make discoveries or suggestions that enhance a programme.

Trainers should let a process go when it has finished, regardless of whether it has yielded the planned points. If, after a reasonable length of time, the magic has failed to work, then it is time to move on to another approach or something different.

All these behaviours and characteristics work to maximize trainees' potential, by developing their respect for the trainer, maintaining the trainer's credibility, and creating confidence in the programme's ability to meet their needs. And none of them will go amiss if copied by trainees in their own work with colleagues, customers and associates.

A five-step model

There is a five-step process that will enable participants to learn any set of skills which are susceptible to good modelling.

1. **Observe excellent practitioners.**
   Ask trainees to note what good performers actually do. If there are a number of experts to consider, what is it that each of them does that is the same? What is it that some do differently? What gives one the edge over another? Find the points of leverage (big gains from small efforts) by considering what is relevant and what is irrelevant.
2. **Hold seminar sessions.**
   Debrief by finding out what the participants have noticed when observing the practitioners. Hear each other's views. Interview or otherwise find out what the experts have to say about their own practices. This is a good place for either the trainer or participants or both to gather and exchange research.
3. **Hold practical sessions.**
   Test good practice in controlled conditions. Do it for real, or use role-plays, simulations and any other participative means to practise these skills. Find out by being and doing. Some of the practices can include side-coaching – that is, the trainer or an expert offering short, helpful suggestions during the practice – or

interruptions. There is a balance to be struck between allowing participants to discover things for themselves and leaving bad habits uncorrected too long.

4. **Reflect on practical experience.**
Feed back after testing. Ask the participants to present their own views of themselves and their colleagues, as well as hearing the views of the trainer or other observers. It can be powerful, if sometimes frightening, to use video recordings so that participants can observe themselves.

5. **Put the skills into practice in the real world.**
Let go, perhaps after a period of observing the learner in the work situation, and allow the trainee to put their learning into practice. Alternatively, provide an iterative – or 'pit-stop' – facility by setting up further reviews after a suitable period. The pit-stop idea should be a very fast check-in to correct any small problems with minimal interruption to the work-flow.

EXPERT MODELLERS

My view is that we are all expert modellers. As a trainer, you can pick up the behaviours and attributes you wish to demonstrate, because you are already familiar with them and no doubt successfully practise them in many areas of your life already. Your participants, too, are used to learning by observing and copying behaviours.

We can demonstrate our expertise in modelling in a process called 'Let's All Be. . .' that is designed to reveal current competence and encourage us to build on that by using our imaginations.

Inspiration works its way into imagination through fantasy. We may suppose that we are the champion, the hero, the expert – or indeed any other role. We have seen others do it, and well. . . next time it could be us.

This, of course, is one of the ways an actor prepares to play a part. An actor is privy to a tremendous insight, gaining an appreciation of what it is like to do what their character does, and knowing – to a degree – what it is like to be that person. In our own performances, we can play at being the expert, the manager, the salesperson and so on. Indeed, if our behaviour is indistinguishable across the required range of circumstances, then it could be argued that we have gone beyond playing and have become the part.

Let's All Be. . . is a game for any number of participants, with no maximum. It can be used for simulating a complete civil war, if that happens to be your requirement. It also functions as:

- an energy-raiser;
- an integrator for teambuilding;
- a stimulus to the imagination.

Let's All Be. . .
State:

'We are going to use the following procedure, and everyone can contribute to it.'

Anyone can say 'I know'.

When someone says 'I know', everyone else responds 'What?'.

The person who initiated 'I know' now says 'Let's all be. . .' and finishes the sentence with a noun or phrase of their choice – perhaps 'Let's all be elephants' or 'Let's all be aeroplanes'.

To this everyone responds, 'Yes, let's all be elephants' (or aeroplanes, or whatever has been proposed).

All group members, including the proposer, then launch themselves into that form of being. If it's elephants, they clomp around heavily, possibly miming trunk action. If it's aeroplanes, they mime flying. If it's accountants, anything can happen. Each piece of action continues until someone else says 'I know'.

The repeating process in this exercise provides structure. Within that, there is a lot of freedom. Any suggestion can be made. All interpretations come from the participants.

When playing Let's All Be. . . with an inexperienced group, you may need to propose quite a few 'I know's near the start to suggest the range of possibilities – 'Let's all be drug-dealers', 'Let's all be gymnasts', 'Let's all be fighting the American civil war' – and to switch fast to maintain energy and enthusiasm.

How long a group chooses to spend on each section within the exercise can vary greatly. Typically, more sophisticated trainees have a greater capacity to stay with a suggestion, and so investigate (and learn from) it more fully. A particularly interesting suggestion may last a long time, creating a totally free-form exploration of 'being', for example, politicians, nuclear reactor molecules or French fishermen. Less sophisticated or inexperienced groups may take time to build their skills to the point where interest holds sufficiently for the game to get beyond the energizing phase.

MODEL STUDENTS

There are limitations to the application of modelling. While behaviours can be copied, the essence of artistry or leadership is always going to prove more elusive. Art is not technique. Situations constantly change, and what works for one person in one circumstance cannot be automatically employed elsewhere. As James P Carse (1986) wrote: 'One does not become an artist by acquiring certain skills or techniques, though one can use any number of skills and techniques in artistic activity. The creative is found in anyone who is prepared for surprise'.

The inspirational trainer, then, is a model of certain qualities and behaviours that prove particularly significant for 'softer' skill programmes. Within some of these programmes, we might explicitly teach modelling as a skill or technique.

Perhaps we might contrast 'trainer-as-model' with 'trainer-as-crowd-control-unit'. The latter – say a teacher in a tough school or a trainer in a jaundiced organization with cynical staff – assumes that the main purpose (and difficulty) of their work is keeping order. Consequently, that is what they spend their time doing. By contrast, the trainer-as-model assumes that everyone is there to learn, and proceeds to teach, model and facilitate as appropriate, allowing crowd control to take care of itself.

The trainer-as-model approach leaves trainees plenty of space to make discoveries for themselves through experiment and playfulness, uninhibited by experts. This imaginative freedom, added to the best elements of traditional masterclass training, makes a powerful combination to prepare for successes back at the workplace.

INSPIRATIONS

- Your knowledge of the content of any topic gives you a head start as a trainer. But you will reap the rewards of that knowledge only if you have the skills to communicate it.
- Know your limitations as an expert, and develop your abilities as a *trainer*.
- Create time for yourself to think, before and during a programme.
- Ask and encourage questions.
- Exercise empathy and humility to put yourself in the most resourceful position for responding authoritatively to the group.

5

The impression of confidence

By harnessing previous experiences of confidence and understanding how to apply them, trainers can be ready to face the most demanding challenges – such as convincing an audience of their credibility even before speaking.

All our good ideas about training will be wasted unless we present ourselves with confidence. We need to be credible to trainees and, without confidence, any credibility with which we start is likely to reduce swiftly to tatters. If we are plausible, and can sustain our plausibility, we stand every chance of successfully delivering the programme.

Some people seem confident and claim they are not. Others maintain that they are, but fail to convince. We each feel different degrees of confidence at different times and in different circumstances. If someone about to give a speech is able to feel as if they were at home, their confidence can be boosted almost miraculously.

When I work with people on their confidence, I prefer to start with inner confidence – that is, the confidence that the person feels. Later we work outwards, considering how confidence is expressed. This approach creates results that last longer and apply to more situations than the 'quick fix' presentational tips that sometimes pass for confidence-building. With inner confidence, your 'fear threshold' is pushed far enough back for you to engage with your students in inspirational learning.

THE RING OF CONFIDENCE

The Ring of Confidence can help us understand and build our own confidence as trainers, as speakers in any circumstances, and serves as a model for teaching confidence to others. Whenever possible, use these quick and effective techniques to enhance trainees' confidence.

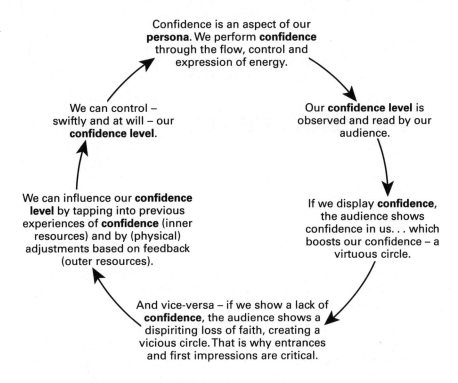

Figure 5.1 *The Ring of Confidence*

Figure 5.1 works as a loop. We might start with the idea: *we can control – swiftly and at will – our confidence level.*

Imagine that confidence can be low or high, on a scale from 0 to 10. The table indicates what each level along the scale might mean to you or to a trainee. We can make the meanings pertinent by recalling specific moments when we actually felt these degrees of confidence. By making the levels personal, we open a channel for tapping into the feelings associated with that level whenever we wish; this helps us to develop the skill of influencing our own confidence levels.

Confidence levels

0. You feel fearful, uninspired, incompetent, listless. The result tends to be inaction until the level rises.
1. You have a minimal feeling of confidence, with every expectation of failure. You lack nerve, so if you pick up a telephone, you might

speak entirely in monosyllables. You have a feeling of being involved when you would prefer not to be. The impression is of defeat, and a phrase associated with this level is 'It's not going to work'.

2. Feeling little hope of success, this is the lacklustre You. When you are doing something, and the phrase 'I really don't expect this to work' goes through your mind, you are at confidence level 2.

3. You have the confidence to function in familiar channels, although you might strike other people as shy or defensive. You keep eye contact to a minimum. Whatever it is you're doing, you believe 'There's a good chance this won't work'.

4. You experience a degree of confidence at which you are comfortable with routine, but hope nothing unexpected occurs. You might put on a reasonable front, but it feels thin and insubstantial. Your inner voice says, 'I doubt if this will work'.

5. At mid-level, you are feeling sufficiently confident to just about manage – if things are average, you reckon you can handle them. Your feeling is that 'This could work'.

6. You can cope and do so competently – though falling short of a flourish. From this level upwards, expectations are positive. After all, 'Maybe it'll work'.

7. You are sufficiently confident to adjust to what immediately confronts you. You are feeling ready to notice and take opportunities. You experience the kind of confidence where you are willing to initiate – perhaps start conversations, put forward ideas, invite someone to sign a contract, feeling 'I trust it will work'.

8. You feel resilient. As well as dealing competently with all routines and having some energy over for new things, you also feel empowered to overcome difficulties or small knocks that tend to accompany challenging activities. Your feeling is expressed by the phrase, 'I expect it will work'.

9. Feeling ready for a spring clean, you take on complex tasks, unswayed by opposition or doubters. You begin that new list of actions with fresh energy. It's time to get it done now because. . . 'I know it'll work'.

10. These are the moments – however brief or long-lived – when you are your own hero, when you feel on your very best form. You feel completely capable of anything, whether frightening, complex or fiendishly difficult. You are 'in the zone'. Level 10 is when you say to yourself – and you mean it – 'I know it cannot fail'.

For feeling confidence now or at the moment when you need it, it is especially helpful to recall instances when you were at levels 10, 9 or 8. Remember how you felt in those circumstances, what emotions you had; sense the way your body was moving, how you looked, how your voice sounded.

Simply tapping into those memories begins to lift your confidence, as your body begins to adopt the confident shape. If you are speaking about such an experience, notice how your voice takes on a confident tone. You are borrowing from your own history, and channelling your own resources – reordering them to equip you again and again.

To influence your confidence level, start by choosing the number you require. You can do this while walking along a busy street, and observe the impact on yourself and those around you. If you choose level 10, and adopt the style, attitude and movements you associate with that level (based on a previous occasion when you felt that way), you will notice very different responses from other pedestrians than if you use the same process with a choice of level 2. Note how you can change levels whenever you wish.

By associating the physical and emotional state with the phrase 'confidence level 10', you can trigger the feeling of confidence at any time you need it by saying 'confidence level 10' and instantly re-entering that state. NLP has a concept called 'anchoring', in which you tie any desired state to a simple trigger. As Anthony Robbins (1988) explains in *Unlimited Power*, his fine introduction to NLP, anchoring is a way to give experience permanence. To be most effective, the trigger or anchor (in this case, saying to oneself 'confidence level 10') should be set up at the moment the emotion is most intensely felt.

PLAYING WITH CONFIDENCE LEVELS

ACTIVITY
Confidence party
Here's how you teach confidence to your participants.

Tell your group you are going to teach everyone how to be more confident. Describe the confidence levels in the table above, adapting the examples for your audience, and point out that any behaviours mentioned are for illustration only. People can behave in any way at any level of confidence. Keep your explanation specific enough for people to be able to relate to it, yet sufficiently vague for them to generate their own images and recollections of confidence at each level.

Tell the participants that they are to interact with each other as if at a social occasion or perhaps at coffee-time before a formal meeting. They may approach or retreat, chat or not, depending on how they are feeling.

Announce that first we will all tap into whatever feeling we associate with confidence level 6, by recalling an occasion when we were engaged in an activity when we felt 'maybe it will work'. Call out a new confidence level every 30 seconds or so. Then ask people to return to their seats, at whatever level of confidence they happen to be feeling, to reflect on what has happened so far.

In this activity, we are each influencing our own confidence level by tapping into a previous experience of confidence. This is an example of using our inner resources, as we apply this feeling to the current activity, namely standing up and mixing with other people in a room.

You can start with any confidence level, but a typical sequence starts with level 6, at which people might diffidently greet each other, perhaps tell each other their names, ask how they are and then move on to talk to someone else. If you then announce 'level 8', in most groups people will move more enthusiastically towards each other, smile as they talk, become more animated. The volume rises. When you call 'level 4', people tend to escape towards the edges of the room. They still speak to each other, but with half-smiles, stutters and hesitations. It is generally quieter.

When feeling confident yourself, you call out 'level 10'. Everyone is suddenly buzzing. Instead of introducing themselves in pairs, often groups of three, four or more, take the initiative in introducing their colleagues to each other. There may be arms round shoulders, high-fives, and sometimes even hugs between previously complete strangers.

After the exercise, it is usually noted that higher confidence levels resulted in higher volumes of communication. Participants often also mention that both physical and eye contact increased, and that they 'felt better' at the higher levels.

Confidence isn't necessarily linked to noise, but the volume will rise in certain settings. For example, if two people are speaking confidently to each other, then the people next to them – feeling equally confident – need to raise their voices slightly to be heard. This makes the first conversation slightly harder to hear but, because the participants are feeling confident, they raise their voices a notch. The feedback loop results in volume rising.

There are ways confidence can be expressed without noise in other social settings. When a group of silent monks reaches confidence level 10 there is no change in volume but there is a palpably different quality to the silence. You could ask your group to imagine that they are silent monks, and to feel confidence level 10. There will be a shift as people sit more upright in their seats. They look more poised, alert, and charged with vitality. The point is that there are many ways of expressing confidence. It is about feeling, not bluster.

In both exercises (when participants are mixing and when they are pretending to be monks) they will have experienced their ability to change instantly, and in the directions they wanted.

Because changing one's level of confidence at will suddenly seems so easy, and the implications strike people as perhaps frighteningly radical or surprisingly powerful, they sometimes seek objections. They say that the exercises are artificial, either because the setting seemed unreal or because they felt they were 'acting'. Some also worry that they won't be able to sustain the technique of changing confidence level, while others are concerned about overconfidence, or whether the technique will work when they want it to – for the speech, in the interview, during the meeting?

These are typical responses when we are trying something new. We are somehow aware of having an insight, or we're uncomfortably conscious that this may mean a rethink, or we recognize a feeling of impending change. Instead of opening ourselves to the experience, we may object, argue or try to dismiss what is happening. I suspect that for many people this is especially true when they are in a group. We may not mind changing, but we don't always want people to watch us doing it. Perhaps it would be preferable as a private process, based on reading an article or book, and then trying it out when only we know what we're doing. A group training situation may create a certain degree of safety, but not always enough to satisfy everyone.

So it is important to deal with objections on their merits. Participants are entitled to check out an insight or plausible new process, to test it and find where it leads. If it is good, it should withstand efforts to disprove it – which is, after all, the scientific method.

To counter the group's doubts, agree that the greetings exercise is a simulation and involves a degree of artificiality. Accept that it can feel quite cumbersome initially to switch levels. But while it may seem awkward at first, that does not alter the fact that changes occurred. Everyone observed switches in his or her own feelings and behaviour and noticed changes in everyone else's behaviour. The alterations were made at the suggestion of the workshop leader and were virtually instant. It was an introduction to a skill that each participant can develop individually at his or her own instigation and at chosen times. Add that practising the skill is likely to make participants more confident people – particularly if they practise it often enough to bring the sorts of successes that help confidence to grow.

I agree with anyone who says they felt they were 'acting': their aim, then, is to become a better actor and act more convincingly. Good actors perform a part with genuine emotion, while knowing simultaneously that they are acting. Their behaviour is intimately connected with the emotions. Playwright George Bernard Shaw reminds us that it is in the nature of acting that we are not to see this woman as Ophelia, but Ophelia as this woman. Some people are splendid natural actors and can draw on the appropriate feelings and behaviours for each circumstance. Acting is 'real' to the extent that it is the presentation of a 'real' persona – a concept explored further below.

Sometimes participants taking part in the exercises put on a very obvious charade of over-the-top pseudo-confidence (for level 10) or whimpering abjectness (for a low level). This is play-acting, and I suggest they try to be as natural and real as possible, given the confidence that they are able to experience at that moment. As comedian George Burns reputedly said, 'Acting is all about honesty. If you can fake that, you've got it made'.

The trainer's energy

As trainers, we can generate an appropriate level 9 or 10 for ourselves, by mixing the characteristics of the calm monks with the excitement and adaptability required for the social setting.

A common factor in the different set-ups so far practised by the groups is energy. Noise is one manifestation of energy, movement is another. It is easy enough to notice the energy of a group. We observe small changes in movement or sound, and soon get a feeling for it. We can sense a silence, feel a stillness.

Constantly gauge the mood of participants, developing your ability to pump energy in, or calm things down, when necessary. Observe how it fluctuates from moment to moment, and know how to influence it through your own actions.

We influence group energy and our own confidence levels through our actions by appreciation of the statement in Figure 5.1 that: *'confidence is an aspect of our persona. We perform confidence through the flow, control and expression of energy'.*

It is the expression of our energy that conveys our level of confidence to the outside world. It is difficult to disguise how we are feeling. If we are low on energy, it is almost impossible to convey high energy for very long.

If we have a great deal of energy, it will emerge somehow. We can observe 'nervous energy' in people when they are about to do something challenging, and when their energy is not completely channelled or controlled. Typically it will leak, perhaps with foot-tapping, or there will be a struggle to suppress it, demonstrated by clenched fists or a tight jaw.

People often confuse what they call 'nerves' with 'lack of confidence'. It is not only possible, but common and quite desirable, for a confident performer to feel nervous immediately before the entrance. The body pulses with adrenaline, which may be experienced as butterflies in the stomach, shakiness or a feeling of nausea. The adrenaline serves as a fuel for the performance itself.

The key in these circumstances is to become familiar with – and accommodate – your own pattern. I know that just before a presentation I usually have an urge to ditch all my prepared material and substitute something else. I also know that it is a good idea for me to keep to the original plan.

The particular ways in which we keep our energy held in or let it out indicate our persona – the way we are in a given circumstance. For example, as a negotiator in a meeting, at a high level of confidence, we might be still, intent on listening, keenly aware of sounds and movements and speak calmly. If it goes badly for some reason and our confidence drops, we might slump a little, start to fidget and hear our voice wavering.

By deliberately changing mental and physical attitudes before business meetings, we can change our business persona. As we do so, others will probably notice we seem more confident, more energized, more flexible and so on. One way of generating this effect is to become aware of the situations in which we feel most confident and transfer the feelings and attitudes from that experience into the setting where we feel less so. If home is a place where I feel confident, I can imagine at meetings that I am at home. I then bring that degree of comfort, relaxation and poise with me to my business meetings.

It is a good idea to imagine that the room in which you speak belongs to you. The audience are welcome guests. It can make a huge difference to the impression you make and how you talk to them. Your tone tends to be friendlier, more welcoming and, in short, more confident. You are borrowing part of your home persona to gain a business advantage, and that behaviour brings the side benefits of increasing the average level of confidence you experience and improving the level of your personal integration. In other words, you can be the same person in more places, with less need to keep changing persona – reducing all the taxing energy demands that the changes impose, such as needing to remember how to be and what you can or can't say in each circumstance.

If we think of a persona as an aspect of ourselves, the challenge is to find that part which enjoys the current activity – whether it is dancing at a party, studying in a library or conducting a training session.

The eye of the beholder

'It used to be said that by the time an Englishman had entered a room and greeted his hostess, every other Englishman would have decided where he came from, where he was educated, how much he earned and how he earned it', writes that astute observer of organizations, Charles Handy.

Our confidence level is observed and read by the audience.

ACTIVITY

Confidence cards

Ask a participant to walk into a room and sit in a chair as if at the start of a meeting or interview. The observers, who sit in an arc facing the chair, have to guess what confidence level the volunteer is experiencing. For most volunteers, the level guessed is close to or exactly that which they are feeling. And in every case, the observers are able to make their guesses instantly.

I use playing cards marked 1–10, showing one to each participant for the first round of guesses. In the second round, I allow each player to choose his or her own confidence level, and the audience and I offer feedback to help players understand and – if they wish – alter the impression they are making.

While level 10 is the most resourceful state, there remains the issue of overconfidence. I believe that overconfidence is not on the same scale but something different altogether, a state in which one cuts oneself off from awareness of what is going on. Overconfidence implies a fixedness, whether it involves either too little or too much preparation, for the event is not treated with the respect it requires.

The person with the loudest voice or most powerful handshake is not necessarily the most confident. Circumstances often favour the quietly confident, wait-and-see approach.

Often the people who ask about overconfidence are those who have been suffering from a lack of confidence. Their question indicates progress in that they are now actively imagining themselves working with higher degrees of confidence. They may fear the consequences of suddenly imposing themselves, appearing too brash or forceful. Well, there is no particular behaviour required by any confidence level; they need not be anything but themselves.

In any event, it is a question of desirability, of selecting what one wants, and having the skill to achieve and present it. If someone believes level 6 is right for a given occasion, they can develop the ability to feel and portray that level. Most trainees realize that level 10 comes in many guises for each person, and they can probably find an excellent means of expressing themselves confidently in the appropriate way for each circumstance.

A trainer working at confidence level 9 or 10 sets up the best possible circumstances for the delivery of the processes and materials. Appearing less confident is generally a disservice to an audience, because it damages their faith in the quality of the training that they are receiving.

One way to check your own mastery of confidence is to observe yourself alone, using a mirror. Like Robert de Niro in the movie *Taxi Driver*, you can practise confidence until you convince yourself that it is safe to go outside, although preferably without the consequent bloodbath. Another approach is to solicit feedback from selected members of a training group, asking them to let you know how you began the session and what impact they felt you made. As in the confidence card activity, feedback should be expressed as observable behaviours, such as 'She made eye contact with almost everyone in the room' rather than 'She looked more confident'. The objective is to explore the particulars which constitute that impression of confidence.

Making an entrance
If we display confidence, the audience has confidence in us. . . which boosts our confidence – a virtuous circle.

And vice versa – if we show a lack of confidence, the audience shows a dispiriting loss of faith, creating a vicious circle. That is why entrances and first impressions are critical.

Everyone knows the phrase 'first impressions', but few remember that the whole expression is 'first impressions are lasting impressions'. The entrance made by the trainer is a significant determinant of how a session is likely to proceed.

The same holds true for an interviewee, for a negotiator or a salesperson, and this is therefore an exercise that you can teach to raise the performance level of participants in a wide range of programmes.

When a trainer enters a room feeling a lack of confidence (let's say level 4), the chances are that the group will read that level fairly accurately –

and instantly. They will react accordingly, by expecting a low-quality session. Now this may not be logical, because the trainer has not said anything at all to indicate whether or not the content will be high quality. We also know that outer expressions are not necessarily linked to inner competence. Nonetheless, if that is how the speaker approaches the platform, the audience will slump in their chairs, look away from the speaker, turn their attention to something else – a newspaper, maybe – and perhaps even start to talk to their neighbour.

Faced with such a set of reactions, the already unconfident presenter now drops a further notch in confidence. The audience responds in turn, and a vicious spiral of ebbing confidence begins. However good the material and delivery from this point on, the trainer has to work hard simply to catch up and regain respect and attention.

Conversely, the trainer entering with confidence level 9 or 10 commands instant respect. The audience believes (again with little real reason) that here is someone who knows their subject. The subconscious belief in the audience may be that the presenter looks confident because the material is under control, but there are many performers with good command of their subject who appear hapless before delivering it, and others who have wonderful presence but little depth of expertise. Members of the audience look attentive, focus on the speaker, and expect the best. Faced with this response, the confident trainer finds confidence reinforced and has a firm platform from which to launch into the material. There is a period of grace, during which confidence is sustained, and even obvious errors may not destroy the faith of trainees.

We can influence our confidence level – by tapping into previous experiences of confidence (inner resources) and by (physical) adjustments based on feedback (outer resources).

Our past experience provides a wealth of inner resources on which we can draw to help us in our present circumstances. As our performance improves, we must note that we did well, in order to allow the accretion of extra confidence. It is all too easy to take our past achievements for granted and dwell only on the slip-ups, mistakes or the tasks we have yet to accomplish. Many people lack confidence because they too readily discount their achievements.

Each of us has a store of confidence. Somewhere in the past we have felt confident entering situations and also while doing things. By bringing these occasions to mind we can be equally confident in new circumstances.

If we haven't felt the necessary confidence level for many months or even years, we should draw on our resources from further back, even searching memories of childhood if that is where the richest storehouse is to be found.

SPACE, STATUS AND SMILES

We can buttress our confidence level by improving other areas of mental preparation. I have already mentioned the idea of thinking of the space as home. Another useful territorial idea is to conceive of the space as belonging to you rather than to the trainees. You can then behave accordingly. You can go where you like: there is no need to retreat defensively behind the nearest desk, and equally no call to propel yourself aggressively into close proximity with the trainees.

A good territorial aim is to find and occupy the focal space. This is in the eyeline of as many people as possible, down the middle line of the room. When you have established that the focal space is yours – mentally rehearsing with the thought 'This belongs to me' – you are free to move in or out of it as you wish. Changing positions occasionally helps keep the trainees' eyes and ears alert.

As long as your movements do not distract trainees from whatever you are saying or intentionally doing, there is no need to keep absolutely still. Too many presentation courses metaphorically strap down the speaker, to the detriment of the speaker's use of energy. If you need to move, move.

Do not, however, jangle coins in your pockets, adjust your spectacles every 40 seconds or continually say 'er'. Any repetitive tic is likely to catch the audience's attention and distract them from your message. To improve as a presenter, become aware of your habits through self-observation, a coach or a video recording. Simply deciding to ditch the habit is a powerful aid. Sometimes it helps to replace a distracting habit with something less intrusive. For example, if you are a throat clearer, try sipping from a glass of water instead.

If you want to maintain a high status as a speaker, avoid short 'er's at the beginning of sentences. In his classic book *Impro* (1981), Keith Johnstone compares the short and long 'er': 'The short "er" is an invitation for people to interrupt you; the long "er" says, "Don't interrupt me, even though I haven't thought what to say yet"'. Johnstone notes that you gain status by keeping your head still and lose it by moving it about or by touching your face with your fingers. Feedback in confidence sessions usually results in tips for polishing the impression you create. These tips are a useful supplement to the power of your inner resources.

Say 'Good morning' as you make your entrance. This puts you into speaking mode and breaks the ice before the potential crunch moment when all eyes are upon you, and you have to speak without the advantage of your body being mobile. I've heard speakers say 'Good morning' two or three times, as if greeting different members or sections of an audience. Later they have revealed that they were surprised at the poor quality of their first utterance and wanted to put their voice into shape before starting their speech.

While interaction has its place, an audience generally expects a platform speaker to be in charge. You can mistime an effort to be friendly and throw away your impression of confidence by asking too many questions that you expect the audience to answer. The audience will feel uneasy under a barrage of 'Everyone OK then? How are you getting on? Ready to start again?'. If you are tempted to ask questions, but don't really want to begin the talk with banter, it is stronger to turn any question that pops into your head into the equivalent statement: 'Good afternoon, what an excellent hotel. Let's get started'. An inspirational touch is to tell a story relating to a point made by a previous speaker or connecting it to an earlier event from the day, making you appear spontaneous and showing that you have been listening.

Making eye contact with members of the audience conveys the message that you are feeling open to communication with them and are not defensive. Eye contact should be varied and, if you feel inhibited about looking directly into the eyes of audience members, then aim slightly above their eye level. Random eye contact seems most natural, so avoid 'machine-gunning' row after row in preordained sequences.

With large audiences, maintain the semblance of eye contact by glancing from section to section. Similarly, if you are so strongly lit that you cannot see the audience, they will still feel you are making eye contact if you look in their direction. It is a tempting mistake to destroy this illusion by shading your eyes from the lights and saying 'I can't see a thing'. Pretend that you can.

Smiling can make a big difference in your favour. It helps to create the emotion of happiness in yourself, as well as reflecting it. Our expressions influence our feelings through subtle mechanics of blood volume alterations and the release of chemicals in the brain.

A great way of winning over an audience quickly is to make them laugh. Again, alluding to something they have just heard or experienced will give the most natural and relaxed impression.

I know some trainers who make their participants laugh without speaking at all. Their secret is to recall immediately before they start the session the last time that they were reduced to helpless laughter. They enter with such *joie de vivre* that the audience can't help but be carried along, confident in the promise of an enjoyable, amusing seminar. It is impossible to force a laugh. And it is unwise to aim for a laugh at your own expense. I heard one speaker begin with 'Can anyone give me a bottle? I've just lost mine', which immediately undercut the audience perception of his confidence level.

The safest assumption is that the audience wants you to succeed and will enjoy whatever you have to say that is of interest and presented in a natural, genuine way.

WARMING UP

Many of the flaws I observe in trainers-as-presenters could easily be eliminated by a warm-up. Athletes and actors warm up as a matter of routine, sometimes for an hour or more. Trainers will typically invest time in preparing notes and visual aids, but consider it eccentric to spend a couple of minutes in warming up their bodies before performing. Yet that is all it takes to avoid a feeble or wooden appearance, and to avoid making excessive adjustments to clothes, throat and props to the amusement of the audience while the talk is going on. A brief warm-up can transform a speaker into a fluent, energized character, ready to take advantage of the virtuous circle of confidence by hitting the stage (metaphorically) running.

There is more information about warm-ups for trainers and their groups in Chapter 8. As a platform speaker, it is also worth paying particular attention to the following:

- **Face** – warm up by giving your face some attention, starting with a soothing temple massage, and ending with a gently invigorating rub around the cheekbones.
- **Mouth** – pretend that you are chewing a large, intractable toffee, very slowly, to exercise your jaw. After about a minute, imagine you have finished but there are sticky bits on your teeth which you need to clean by stretching and twisting your tongue. Now practise a smile by imagining you are happy.
- **Hands** – encourage your energy to flow freely around your hands by shaking them from the wrist for two bursts of about 30 seconds. The faster the shake the better, so aim for an invisible blur. All dropped hand jewellery belongs to the trainer.
- **Breathing** – you can use deep breathing to calm yourself or rapid, shallow breathing to excite yourself. Breathe according to your needs and, whichever breathing pattern you choose, use it to focus on your breath as a way of centring yourself before the presentation.
- **Voice** – vocal preparation may be slightly trickier than other warm-ups to accomplish in privacy. If you do get the chance, singing is a good way to prepare your voice for a talk.
- **Mirror check** – check in a mirror before you begin your session. This will confirm that you are looking good and give you a final chance to observe your smile and adjust any element of your appearance which might detract from the impression you wish to create.

PRESENTING WITH STYLE

Confidence is an important tool of inspirational training in that it equips a trainer to play with all the elements of a presentation. You can change speed deliberately. You can note bad habits and eliminate them. Timing is under your control. You can create rhythms, and break them – possibly using irregular timing to keep the audience's attention and keep yourself alert.

As you make choices, you will widen your range of gestures and actions, discovering what works best to illustrate your words. Making these choices keeps your awareness present in your body, alert to the needs of the group, and will sustain your performance on any platform.

INSPIRATIONS

- Confidence is the foundation of your authority and credibility as a trainer.
- Confidence is something you can do, as well as have. Doing confidence is a skill you can develop for yourself – and teach to your participants.
- Assume that your audience wants you to succeed and will give you the benefit of the doubt.
- Warm up, smile, make eye contact and find that part of yourself which enjoys being up front.

6

Learning to apply

Gain cooperation and better results by understanding how to motivate participants. What's in it for them? Clarify the elements that they can enjoy during the programme and the benefits to take back to their organizations.

The main point of training is for trainees to know their subject and/or be able to perform their functions better. If it is well targeted, then the right people will be learning the right things. What remains is for them to take new knowledge and skills into their regular lives. This, in short, is the issue of transferability.

Some programmes fail because trainees never have a chance to use their training back at base. This may be due to the organization's structure. Many cultures resist change. 'The Way Things Are Done' cannot easily be altered by one or two individuals returning from an inspirational training event.

Lack of transfer may also arise because participants have not properly considered how to implement their learning. It is an integral part of the programme for the trainer to direct participants' attention to transferability. Training is learning not for its own sake but for some purpose. Inspirational training demands motivated candidates – and awareness of usefulness is a powerful motivator for many people.

INCLUDE USEFULNESS ON THE AGENDA

As a minimum, ask: 'How and when are you going to use the skills, insights and knowledge you are gaining?'. Questions about implementation are strongest when they are:

- implicit at the objectives stage;
- woven into exercises and processes;

- given a section of their own (action planning and action points);
- explicitly addressed when considering obstacles to implementation.

Note whether the stated programme objectives or the participants' objectives refer to the application of skills and/or knowledge. If our trainees' objectives make no mention of applying new learning, we can legitimately question what the programme is for. There may be merit, for example, in learning skills for the sake of it, whether or not we find applications later (although it is increasingly hard to find sponsors for such 'pure' learning). The point is to be aware of the purpose and to avoid the feeling of a course running in a vacuum.

I have attended courses where I learnt skills I was unable to apply immediately. The danger was that they would atrophy while I waited for the chance to put them into practice. On one occasion the gap between good and actual management practice in my place of work was made so apparent by the training that I left the organization. Perhaps a better-designed course would have warned me to expect the lack of opportunity or helped me discover ways of bringing my new learning to bear that I had missed. If so, my expectations would have been more realistic. Or perhaps the training philosophy was simply more advanced than the employer's practices – often the case in large organizations.

From the organization's point of view, it makes sense to ensure that trainees will have an opportunity to put training into practice. Armed with new skills and ideas, they may be heading for increased responsibilities and promotion – or frustration and departure.

For the trainer, finding ways to enable skills-transfer from the training environment to the workplace or elsewhere in life is generally an important – yet surprisingly often forgotten – objective of a programme.

First check whether the objectives of your programme are congruent with the aims of the trainees' organizations. Will the objectives, when achieved, be directly or indirectly useful? An example of a directly useful objective would be the ability to use a firm's new financial software package. An indirectly useful objective might be the development of life skills, such as influencing or listening skills, so that companies are inhabited by more competent individuals who will work more effectively with colleagues.

Ask participants to imagine themselves using the achieved objectives: if their answers include realistic organizational scenarios, you are on the right track.

EMOTIONAL INVOLVEMENT

Within a training event, participants are likely to engage in some processes which may not initially seem directly related to the objectives. Sometimes it is sufficient for the trainer to know why each element of a programme is included; sometimes participants are more comfortable if they also know. Most groups are satisfied when told that everything should make sense eventually and that some processes are designed to be run without them knowing exactly what they are about beforehand.

From time to time, redirect attention towards objectives and transferability. For example, when trainees begin to display new skills and understandings, we can use the impetus of their success. A simple, effective technique is to use action points within an action plan to look forward to implementing new learning.

Future perspective

If you keep your participants informed and busy with a variety of activities, the course itself will prove enjoyable. A sense of purpose beyond the course will provide an extra motivational impetus to the benefit of the course while it is running.

Motivation is more difficult when participants are facing an uncertain or bleak future. While participants' attitudes towards their work may not concern us directly, our success hinges on good motivation during the course. Without it, little learning will occur, which means appreciating that some programmes will work only when we help participants grapple with issues that concern them beyond the course.

One method is explicitly to encourage trainees to think about the upside and downside of possible futures. Some people are motivated more by positive aspects, others by negative. The former are motivated by the benefits of moving towards the goal. We state the goal, and help people appreciate what is in it for them. Negatively-motivated people need to know the pains and horrors of what's going to happen (preferably to them) if there is no change, or if we move away from the goal. This is especially significant if participants fear the results of the programme itself, as can happen with strategic summits about mergers, downsizing, retooling and other radical change. Even facing the worst possibilities – such as the loss of one's own job – can bring some comfort. Once participants have considered the bottom line, there is the potential for acceptance and moving on.

In any motivational project it is wise to cover both the positive and negative to ensure we reach all candidates. By making the two possible future strands (positive and negative) vivid in the mind, we become motivational artists, clarifying the dilemmas from which our students can make their own choices.

NSPIRATIONS

Creating a scenario for motivation

First show that change is inevitable, and the status quo is not an option:

When dealing with positive motivation

- Stress the benefits of change for the person involved.
- Offer examples where such change has worked well for others.
- Create a vivid, detailed scenario of the future.

When dealing with negative motivation

- Introduce the bad consequences as quickly as possible to speed up the changes.
- Where possible, create images and samples of these consequences.

You might make a strong impact by taking your group to visit two sites – a modern exemplar of best practice and a derelict factory, say, which failed to heed warnings similar to those which they are facing. A visit makes more impact than a video, which may be more impressive than a still picture, which is preferable to a detailed description, which beats a vague warning.

GOALS

Studies consistently show that people with goals perform at higher levels than people without goals. Poet Robert Browning captures the inspirational nature of striving with his lines, 'Ah, but man's reach should exceed his grasp, Or what's a Heaven for?' (1845).

If, within a training programme, you can prompt participants to set themselves goals, they are likely to achieve more than if you (or the sponsor) set the goals for them. Motivation to achieve an objective which you have set yourself is far stronger than any external stimulus. Personal goals are more likely to be perceived as serving one's own interests than management goals. Once someone has accepted a goal, commitment is strengthened by taking the first action towards it, such as writing it down or telling somebody else.

Depending on the programme, you might ask participants to differentiate between goals which they plan to achieve during the programme and those to be achieved afterwards. Confidence is progressively raised as each goal is reached. Motivation is stronger when:

- a goal is written down;
- there is a public commitment to a goal;
- there is a consideration of likely obstacles;
- there is a plan to overcome the obstacles.

Note that actually achieving the goal is not always the most significant part of the process. For some people, falling short of a goal matters little – they appreciate their effort and accomplishments along the way. For others the joy is in reaching it, and some take most pleasure in surpassing their goals. Nevertheless, in each case, having the goal remains paramount.

Researchers Sims and Lorenzi (1992: 117) write: 'Effective performers, although they may be driven by goals, do not always fully attain their goals. . . The emphasis is on improved performance, not goal attainment *per se*'. A specific goal is more effective for managing performance and evaluating results than an ambiguous 'do your best' goal. So encourage participants to be precise in their wording. One good test is whether the goal implies an evidence procedure. Can the goal-setter explain how they would know or show that the goal had been achieved?

Because they contain an element of challenge, difficult yet attainable goals lead to higher performance than easy goals. The trainer's job is to create a climate in which each participant is inspired to set high personal expectations.

Why do goals work?
Goals:

- focus attention;
- prompt action;
- mobilize effort;
- create persistence, ie directed effort over a period of time;
- lead to strategy developments – there may be several routes to the goal.

EXPECTATION AND SUPPORT

Each goal can be buttressed by mini-goals, deadlines and action plans. If my goal is to write a book, one point in my action plan might be to write at least 300 words every day. This breaks the large task down into smaller, more manageable chunks. I can work like a journalist, with a series of deadlines – effective daily prompts.

In my courses for writers, I encourage participants to set a daily target. When they discover that they can achieve it, they appreciate the power of the deadline as a way of maintaining motivation and production when the backing of a current training programme has ended.

While goals prompt and develop motivation, *sustained* motivation generally requires support. A trainer can help people to succeed by supporting, as well as challenging them. This is one reason why feedback and follow-ups are important elements in your programmes. By monitoring how people are doing, you discover the necessary levels of support.

Figure 6.1 *The expectation–support model*

We use this model to analyse what is needed to create and maintain the most fruitful tension between the axes for enabling inspirational learning to take place. If we are teaching motivation, trainees can apply the model to their own circumstances by filling in a blank version.

Consider what characterizes each quadrant. The bottom right quadrant depicts an organization where support is high and expectation low. We might predict a lazy atmosphere, with personnel feeling safe and cosy. Because little is expected, little is achieved. If there are targets, they are low. This is the paternalistic culture of the civil service, traditional family firms or local government, characterized by the assumption of 'jobs for life'. If the atmosphere of safety persists when conditions outside the organization become ruthlessly competitive, there can be fatal consequences. Disaster can often be foreseen and avoided, but only if the signs are recognized early enough. In Charles Handy's classic example (1989), a frog in a pan of water which is slowly heated fails to jump out and is boiled because the change is so gradual.

To the bottom left we have low expectation and low support, generating feelings of apathy, being stuck, and decline. These feelings can apply to individuals or be redolent of a whole department or organization. Some- times we can stimulate insight by asking people to place their department on the grid and then, for comparison, plot their own personal life position.

Top left is high expectation and low support, creating stress and burn- out, in an atmosphere targeted on results and crackling with pressure. Although high expectation sometimes inspires people to go out and achieve, without the necessary resources the cost in morale and staff turnover could be high. Setting lofty targets without back-up is a recipe for disappointment.

The top right, where both expectation and support are high, is character- ized by achievement, with results engendered by fair challenge. When filling in this quadrant, students include 'cooperation', 'getting things done', 'excitement', 'results' and even 'awesome'.

The model is prescriptive as well as diagnostic. Any position plotted on the chart implies recommendations of what to do to increase effectiveness. If we want to aim, say, for the top-right quadrant, we first assess where we are now. It is then apparent whether we need to increase expectation or support. Inspirational learning takes place when trainees experience the challenge of expectation combined with the safety of support.

This is a good time, in a seminar on motivation, to split the participants into groups and ask them to devise proposals for actions that they can themselves take to bring the diagram into organizational reality. This exercise combines analysis with creative, practical thinking, plus a touch of competition. It also frequently results in transferable ideas with partic- ipants committed to fruitful specific actions, both on their own and cooperatively.

MUSES AND ANTI-MUSES

Motivation is personal, and the trainees themselves often know best the conditions that they need for learning. The next activity helps them articulate the circumstances which will help them to transfer, reinforce and develop the skills from a training event.

ACTIVITY

Muses

Remind the participants that the classical poets wrote only when inspired by the Greek goddesses known as the muses. The participants' challenge is to explore their self-knowledge and imagination to generate a long list of their own muses that they will be able to use to motivate themselves. Later they might adapt the process to motivate others.

Explain that muses appear in many guises. For some poets, their muse is the presence of a certain woman; for others it is a glass of fine port. Whatever conditions create the atmosphere in which they can accomplish the task in question – whether that is writing, managing your team, getting on with your task – can be considered their set of muses. Their list should incorporate all dimensions that have an effect on them. Where do they like to be, what do they like to be present, what sounds, what temperature, what time of day do they prefer?

Next ask them to list their anti-muses – everything that prevents them from making a start or that successfully interrupts them once they have got going.

I have heard a wide range of muses and anti-muses, including particular foods, specific brands of writing paper, the need for solitude – and for company. Often people surprise themselves with their lists and are able to use them to make significant changes. As someone said in one workshop, 'I hadn't realized that I only write at night. That's limiting my opportunity to get much written'. The next step, of course, is for participants to engineer events to incorporate their muses and to eliminate the anti-muses.

Finally, warn of the danger of being too accepting of the current range of muses, as we can sometimes end up in their thrall. It is better to discover some new ones. Many writers and managers have increased their output three- or four-fold by timely manipulation – and extension – of their muses and anti-muses.

LEADERSHIP AND VISION

Motivation may come from within, but we also seek it from outside sources – particularly from leaders. There are times when you will need to be the leader of your training programme. If you sense reluctance in others to participate, for example, you will have to take the initiative. At other times it is enough to facilitate, allowing others to be in the forefront.

Catherine The Great once said that a good leader tells the people to do what they were going to do anyway. Taking this wisdom from Russian history and applying it to today's training programmes, we may assume that it will be a losing battle to try to lead people where they have no intention of going.

The harmonious style of leadership takes existing inclinations into account and requires an awareness of current organizational culture. For instance, if a company sets all its bonus systems to reward the individual, then isolated efforts to lead them towards teamwork are likely to fail. If, however, the aims of our programme accord with the organization's committed objectives, then the stage is set for a vital ingredient of leadership – vision.

Vision is the image of the destination. The leader's role is to make that image vivid in the minds of those who are heading there. Whether the details of the vision are conjured up by the leader alone or through a participative process, they result in a common purpose. The key to leadership is to find ways of articulating the vision and remind followers of it whenever necessary. For the purposes of inspirational training, the trainer will be aware of the vision, and can bring it to the forefront from time to time. It means having a sense of how each part of the programme fits the whole.

The purpose of a vision is to inspire. It helps the leader by energizing a group of people around a set of values: 'This is what we are trying to achieve, and it is a worthwhile aim'.

Within the vision, each individual then has a part to play, contributing in distinctive ways. When leadership is working well, everyone involved advances towards taking charge of their own destiny. As individuals, we become confident and empowered, with the leader taking particular responsibility to ensure against the danger of people pulling in different directions. During training, this might mean devising processes that result in participants generating practical ways of realizing separate and joint visions.

Once the vision is in place, the best ways for leaders to improve the performance of their followers – and for trainers to help trainees – include:

- asking people to behave in the ways you want them to;
- encouraging and praising;
- noticing people doing something right;
- giving feedback, and other 'rewards', along the way – promptly, in response to the behaviour you want, proportionately and in ways which are valued by the recipients.

ACTION PLANS AND ACTION POINTS

From the outset, encourage trainees to consider what they are going to do with new skills, knowledge and insights when they are back in the workplace. Anything they decide to do can be recorded – at the time of decision – as an action point. This means writing the points down (at least in draft) as the programme progresses.

A written action point is likely to be more useful in a number of ways than mere mental notes. The writing not only serves as a record – to aid memory – but also as compelling, undeniable physical evidence of intent.

A set of action points makes up an action plan. Action plans range from precision tools which look set to galvanize entire organizations to vague wish-lists which have a minimal chance of making any difference to anything. There is clearly little point in an action plan which fails to lead to action, so encourage the participants to check each point against the acronym MATER:

> **M**easurable
> **A**ctive
> **T**imed
> **E**gotistical
> **R**eachable

Measurable means that the action point should be couched in specific terms. It may be to do 20 press-ups, make 12 phone calls or improve productivity by 5 per cent. Avoid non-specific words, such as 'some', 'a few', or anything vague that can be made more concrete. The 'sharpening question' seeks the measurement. It may be 'How many?' 'How often?' or simply 'What measurement do you have in mind here?' 'One' and 'All' are often good answers.

Make action points Active. It may sound obvious, but you would be amazed how many so-called 'action points' avoid the cumbersome necessity of doing anything at all. 'My department will be ready for the next budget round' begs all the questions about how. Use active or 'doing' words. Imagine that an observer could see the action take place, and would definitely notice if it was not happening.

Timed means that there is a time, date or occasion by which it can be judged whether or not the action has been taken. 'I shall do it by Tuesday'; 'It will be ready before the next meeting'. Time creates deadlines, which have great motivating qualities for many people.

Actions need to be Egotistical: they are to be carried out by the person who makes the point. Action points generally start with 'I'. They commit the protagonist to doing something. 'I shall run to work', 'I shall meet the supervisor'. It is no use creating action points which you expect others to carry out. That is another subject altogether.

Finally, all targets should be Reachable. It is good for them to be challenging or stretching, but if they are unfeasible or clearly beyond capability, they will probably prove counter-productive. A challenging action point which you fail to achieve may be fine. If you almost reach a personal target, you may feel satisfaction, and it may also exceed a target which someone else has set.

Surprisingly, small new actions can prove the most significant of all. Rather than seeking the greatest reachable target, set an action which is easily within your scope, but which could make a significant difference on account of its symbolic value or its knock-on effects which alter everything else in a system. My advice, when deadlocked, is to use the leverage principle and make a small shift.

Action points which start with expressions such as 'I intend to. . .' or 'I'll try. . .' are weak, and the trainer should ask the participant to rephrase them as 'I shall. . .'.

You can make participants aware that they might run into difficulties in their efforts to carry out their actions. Some preparatory thought at this time about how to overcome obstacles pays dividends. The obstacle may be any area of difficulty surrounding the action. An action point such as 'I shall ask the head of the department on Monday to increase the IT budget for next year by 25 per cent' could run into obstacles at either end. It may be tricky to arrange the meeting, to overcome one's inhibitions about making the request, or there may be a prior need to prepare good reasons to support the case.

It is useful to ask partners or small groups to share action plans. Sharing encourages clarification – particularly if we allow sharpening questions, as described above. Also, a public statement of intention increases the likelihood of that intention being acted upon. If possible, include a public statement of a selection of goals (perhaps one per person) to the whole group. Again, there is the benefit of public commitment, plus a strong chance of collective motivation – whether through inspiration, competition or embarrassment.

The nature of action points is that they can easily be checked: either the action has or has not been taken in the time allowed. So it is important to arrange for feedback and checking, preferably in a follow-up session dedicated to examining, recalibrating and celebration. If a formal follow-up proves impossible, ask the trainees to put a date in their diaries to do their own action plan check and update.

Many people tend to undervalue and dismiss their achievements. At the time the plan was made, the points may have seemed ambitious. By the time the group meets again and the actions have been taken, it may seem no big deal. As trainers we can remind participants of just how much significant progress has been made. A collection of achieved action points – written and posted on a wall – can be an impressive and inspiring sight. It sets the stage for everyone to make an updated plan in which they can, of course, be even more ambitious if they wish.

On the rare occasions when no action has been taken, there is usually a good reason. Circumstances may have changed – sometimes for the better. In any case, there is opportunity to revise and set new goals and actions.

ATTITUDE: THE CHAT SHOW GAME

Attitude is the final key to transferability. Many despondent managers complain about workers' negative attitudes. They feel that their staff have the wrong approach to the job and that a change in attitude is the key to improvement. The following exercise, the Chat Show Game – a sequence of interviews, borrowing the format of a television or radio show – will amuse and inspire them. It is also a valuable sequence to use when your explicit objective is to shift trainees' attitudes.

ACTIVITY

The Chat Show Game

Introduce the activity by calling it after whoever serves as the resonant chat-show host or hostess for your group. It is suitable for large numbers as well as small gatherings, and you start by dividing the group into pairs. It can alternatively be run with trios, with the third person as observer/referee, if you want to stress observable aspects through feedback. Generally, though, the biggest impact comes from people learning during their own improvisations and noting the lessons of the game for themselves.

Player A in each pair is the eponymous interviewer, whose job is to ask Player B, the guest on the programme, all about what is going on in the department/organization/guest's life, and to find out how that is affecting their guest. Alternatively, the interview can be about one forthcoming important event, about which the protagonist might have one attitude or another.

In round one, the guest's job is to answer the questions with as negative an attitude as possible. The idea is to remain plausible, but

---

take a pessimistic view, so that whenever there is an equal chance of success or failure at any step along the way, it is the negative path that is followed.

The interviewer must accommodate the attitude – neither lead nor contradict it. The focus is on consequences – finding out what will happen as the guest's situation unravels. If the interviewer reaches the end of a chain of events, then it is time to tackle another aspect of the subject.

It might go like this:

A   Welcome to the show, Henry Nash, finance director of Petulike Petfoods. Tell us about what's happening at work.

B   *Well, the main thing, Selina, is that the department is being reorganized, and it's possible I'll be out of a job.*

A   Out of a job?

B   *Yes, I reckon so. They're losing half of us and the chances are that I'll be among them.*

A   Will it be a random selection process?

B   *No, there will be a series of appraisal interviews and, depending on past performance, ideas for the future and the needs of the department, the selection will take place accordingly. So it's looking pretty grim for me.*

A   Why's that?

B   *Well, I can't see much of a future for myself there. I've made a couple of slip-ups in the past. One or two of them still remember the canteen cup fiasco of '98. And the new candidates have very strong qualifications.*

A   When will you be leaving?

B   *Two or three months. I suppose I'll sit at home for a while, then wonder what to do. Spend some of the redundancy package.*

A   Get another job?

B   *Well, that's debatable. There's a lot of unemployment. Quite a hassle to look for work. And I don't see the point in filling in loads of application forms if they're going to be a waste of time.*

A   So what will the impact be at home?

B   *It could cause a lot of tension between me and my wife. She works from home and with me under her feet she'll get agitated. Could affect her business quite badly. And without the income the pressures are going to be unbearable. When the redundancy money goes, there's every chance we'll split up.*

A   What would you do then?

B   *There's some friends I haven't seen for a while. Maybe I could stay with them. Though probably not. They won't have the space. I could try begging on the streets. I can't juggle or play a guitar.*

Depending on the group (and to a lesser extent the situation), the interviewee will often be approaching suicide within a few minutes, by which time you should be ready to call a halt. Ask the interviewers to wind up the interview with a closing question and to thank the guests for appearing on the show.

To complete round one, the pair swap chairs and roles, with B as the interviewer and A as the guest.

On the other hand. . .

In round two, the scenario is the same. A is the interviewer again, and takes the interviewer's chair. The only difference is that this time B is to answer with a positive attitude, putting the better gloss on the answers.

A Welcome to the programme, Henry Nash, finance director of Petulike Petfoods. Tell us what's happening at work.

B *Well, the main thing, Selina, is that the department is being reorganized and all the jobs are up for grabs.*

A So you could be out of a job?

B *Well, that is possible, but half the positions are open, so I fully expect to pick up one of those.*

A Will it be a random selection process?

B *I'm glad to say there will be a series of appraisal interviews and, depending on past performance, ideas for the future and the needs of the department, the selection will take place accordingly. So it's looking pretty good for me.*

A Why do you say that?

B *I can point to my excellent record and all the achievements which I've been part of. The profit record has been consistently good, and the senior management have noted my contributions, formally and informally, verbally and in writing. Along with my experience, I've plenty of ideas on where we can go from here with a new lean-look department.*

A What if you get one of these posts?

B *It will be a great boost. Changing positions within a completely reorganized team will give me a whole new perspective. There's a new computerized cash-flow projection system I want to suggest, which will enable our support role to be even stronger.*

A Will it make any difference to your personal life?

B *My wife is always saying I need a new challenge. And if I feel revitalized in the office, then it's going to pep up the home life too. With our joint incomes, we can take that exotic holiday we've been promising ourselves.*

A I'm not really supposed to ask you this, but just supposing you didn't get the job?

B *No problem. Part of my preparations will be to list all my transferable skills and to find out how I compare in the current jobs market. There are loads of organizations which could benefit from my skills and experience. And I'm quite tempted to float a few applications around anyway – just to test the waters.*

Again, to complete the round, the interviewer and guest swap places, and A has the opportunity to paint a scenario with a positive attitude.

Now reveal the diagram:

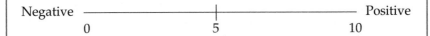

Negative ————————————————— Positive
0   5   10

and say, 'While I appreciate that you have been working towards the extremes on this line, with the negative attitude represented by somewhere near zero and the positive close to 10, perhaps you have a sense of where your usual attitude appears on the scale. Breaking it down further, where you would score your attitude within the department, the organization, your home?'.

Participants find it valuable to chart their scores on a public graph if the attitude of the team as a whole is at issue. Otherwise, allow trainees to keep their findings confidential, letting their own realization of the possible consequences of their attitude make an impact.

Then ask what the participants believe are the consequences of holding attitudes at either end of the scale. Do they, for example, believe that taking a certain attitude makes any difference to the outcome?

Usually the group furnishes examples of a positive attitude leading to success and a negative attitude to failure. You might reinforce the point by mentioning the power of visualization as a proven technique for top performers in sport, business and the arts. The participants have effectively completed a pair of visualizations – journeys with self-generated imagery – of possible paths they could follow.

Like our confidence level, our attitude is within our control – a skill which we can develop through processes such as visualizations and the Chat Show game.

One facet of this skill is to maintain a personal attitude different from that within a group. It is hard to stay positive in a negative group, or negative amongst a positive crowd. Group mindset is pervasive, and takes a special effort to shift or escape.

PERSONAL FLEXIBLE FUTURES

These tools of transferability help participants create their own flexible futures. Spadework during the training programme produces fruits for the organization.

As trainers we should remember that our own attitudes are an influential model. If we remain positive about the processes within our training programme, and about the likely benefits to participants beyond the course, we shall consistently create conditions for motivating and bringing out the best in our trainees.

NSPIRATIONS

- Training is learning for a purpose – and so it needs to transfer from the training room into the arena of application.
- Ask participants regularly how they will apply or implement their learning.
- People with goals perform better than people without goals. Make sure the goals are challenging, achievable and written down.
- Make sure there is support as well as expectation.
- A trainer's vision of where a course is heading can inspire and energize, creating the strategies and attitudes which enable trainees to reach their targets.

7

Creative principles

Now you can apply an array of creative principles to the design of your programmes. These will increase your effectiveness, ensure you reach every learner, and make work more like play.

Variety is central to inspirational training. Changes of style and pace are antidotes to boredom, and each person has a unique way of learning, responding differently to the various methods of teaching. The trainer must therefore use a range of styles to accommodate each learner's preferences.

Recent research provides insight into the ways in which we best learn. The findings indicate benefits for trainers who can apply new under-standings about left-brain and right-brain preferences, sensory strengths and more diverse concepts of intelligence.

BRAINS AND INTELLIGENCE

The two-sided brain

From the pioneering discoveries of experimenter Roger Sperry and other scientists involved in cranial research, we know that the brain has two hemispheres which have broadly distinctive functions, yet work in harmony. Using both sides together enhances academic and creative success.

While traditional teaching is directed towards left-brain strengths, valuing ever more precise points of linguistic or mathematical finesse, inspirational training offers equal respect to the right brain. The sensitive trainer will endeavour to engage both 'sides' of participants' brains with a variety of activities and approaches.

This holistic approach develops each individual's complete set of talents. Here are some simple yet effective ways of creating harmonious education:

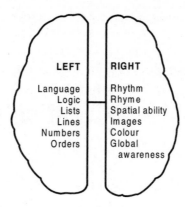

Figure 7.1 *The two-sided brain*

- **Show the big picture first.** At the start of a programme, give the participants a summary of the content. This could be in poster form, with appropriate pictures and symbols; with key words on the poster; and with a description no longer than a couple of sentences.

    Similarly, at the start of each significant session offer a big picture to orient the learner's right brain. Without the overview, the right brain is lost. A colleague was so distressed by the absence of introductory summaries in one of my wife's books that he was unable to read it, despite agreeing with almost all of its sentiments. Left-brain-dominated learners won't mind the brief introduction, and can then tackle the detailed logical sequences which follow.
- **Use colour in posters, handouts and display materials.** Colourful materials are more attractive, distinctive, memorable, stimulating and emotional.
- **Play music.** Include a song – pre-recorded or sung by participants, depending how adventurous they are feeling – to coordinate both sides of the brain, words stimulating the left, music the right.

People learn in different ways

We take in our information through our five senses. The senses can be understood as learning channels.

The largest proportion of your participants will learn best visually, responding to pictures, colour and reading. Auditory learners remember what they hear. They prefer to listen to information, through lectures, tapes and discussion. Kinaesthetic learners need to move, learning best through their bodies – with activities, actions and hands-on approaches.

Taste and smell feature strongly in certain environments, involving food, chemicals, wine, paint, flowers and perfumes. For most training purposes, taste and smell have limited applications. Smells can be particularly intrusive and distracting, so aim to keep training environments fresh, smoke-free and aired.

When you are coaching one-to-one, it may be worthwhile to concentrate on your learner's strongest channel. But in a class or group setting, make sure there is plenty to see, hear and touch, to create a rich learning environment.

Keep a sense of purpose

One training event I attended featured an exercise in which our syndicate group was asked to list interesting aspects of our training centre and hotel. It proved impossible for us to agree on how to do this task until we agreed on the purpose. Who or what was this information for? Once we decided it was for ourselves (an easy choice perhaps), we could proceed.

For individuals to benefit from training, they must each appreciate the purpose of the course, that the course has meaning and use for them, and that each sequence within the programme fits – in some way, however obscure – the overall sense of purpose.

During writing skills courses, we spend time doing a visualization. It may seem odd or irrelevant at first, so I explain that the purpose is to help writers in the essential task of finding exactly what inspires them to write.

MULTIPLE INTELLIGENCES AND THE 'GRAIN OF THE BRAIN'

Psycholinguist Noam Chomsky suggests we are pre-disposed to accept information in certain patterns – such as language or music – and that this is the way we construct our knowledge. Language and music are not merely expressions of the way the human brain works; their forms and grammars are 'inbuilt' and occur universally wherever humans exist. If this is the case, we should take advantage of these pre-dispositions in our design of training programmes, easing the way for ourselves and our learners by working with the 'grain of the brain'.

The work of Dr Howard Gardner, who introduced the idea that we have at least seven intelligences, is developed by Linda Campbell, Bruce Campbell and Dee Dickinson (1995). They define intelligence as:

- the ability to solve problems that one encounters in real life;
- the ability to generate new problems to solve;
- the ability to make something or offer a service that is valued within one's culture.

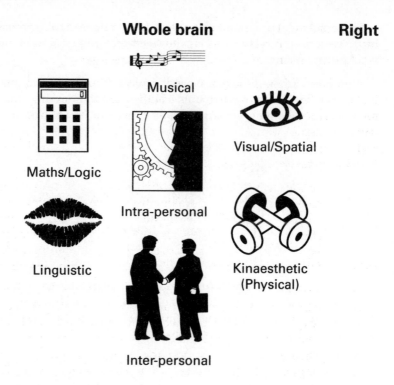

Left   **Whole brain**   **Right**

Musical

Maths/Logic

Intra-personal

Visual/Spatial

Linguistic

Kinaesthetic (Physical)

Inter-personal

Figure 7.2 *Seven intelligences*

Gardner allows for more than seven intelligences, some researchers split visual and spatial into two separate intelligences. And I know what you're thinking: what about intuition? Could our sixth sense be the eighth intelligence?

By designing processes deliberately to appeal across all the intelligences at some time or other, you ensure that the message reaches all learners. It is both economical and efficient to combine the intelligences you address in any one process.

Let us take in turn the seven intelligences identified in Figure 7.2 and consider how we might use them to engage trainees.

Linguistic intelligence
This involves thinking in words. We develop it through talking, listening, reading and writing.

During short courses, encourage delegates to read short pieces of inform- ation, briefings or sets of instructions to themselves. Other information may be fun to read aloud, perhaps prompting discussion.

On a residential programme, suggest that people read background books, pamphlets, magazines and each other's reports in their spare time. These are a fruitful source of information for many learners.

Sometimes whole-group discussion is valuable, although I often sense irritation when certain participants feel the talk is wandering. You can opt for discussion in pairs or small groups, perhaps structured to tackle a particular issue or for sharing a specific type of experience. One or more in each group can be asked to listen, reflect, support, or listen and report back, perhaps by taking notes and summarizing.

Dr Lyman Steil, at the University of Minnesota, calculates that individuals spend about 80 per cent of their waking hours communicating, and 45 per cent of that time listening. This implies advantages for anyone who develops effective listening strategies. At present, Steil contends that we typically recall only half of what was said in a ten-minute talk, and lose 25 per cent of that in next 48 hours – even if we are keen to remember.

One way to develop learners' listening skills is to ask participants to write down what they already know about a subject before you start. They should include any questions which they would like answered. In this way, they prepare to listen actively. During the talk, keep the participants' attention by asking them to outline or mindmap significant points or to jot down questions or points of interest. They will listen purposefully.

Encourage all participants to speak by ensuring a rough equality of opportunity. You can encourage everyone to speak by taking turns – in a circle, for example, or by use of a 'talking talisman', a ball, stick or other item which is held by the speaker and passed on, making it apparent if anyone is dominating the discussion or interrupting the talisman holder. This method is regularly employed in primary schools.

Other activities that encourage linguistic intelligence are writing poems, inventing slogans and conducting interviews. Any of these can help identify and express concerns, ideas, attitudes and solutions.

Logical–mathematical intelligence
This intelligence involves order, calculation, quantification, hypothesizing and analysis.

You can tap into and develop it by asking people to justify statements, to look for patterns and connections in diverse phenomena, and to observe and investigate the subjects in question.

Perhaps you have information that can be presented in Venn diagrams or graphs or tables. I have seen a lecturer struggle to explain a concept to a participant with a strong logical–mathematical intelligence. As soon as he produced a simple graph, the concept became miraculously clear.

If you want trainees to discover things for themselves in a scientific mode, ask them to design and conduct an experiment – clearly a classic means for learning, whether on a small, informal scale or in the grand manner of scientific institutions. Participants begin to reach the heart of communication skills, for example, when comparing the reactions of colleagues to respectful listening and to normal conversation.

Find activities involving numbers and measurements to appeal to this intelligence. One approach is to gather a selection of points relating to your subject and name them 'The Five Keys. . .' or 'The Seven Steps. . .'.

Many organizational and production problems have been solved in workshops where participants are invited to devise improved sequences. One employment agency, for example, used to call clients in a certain order, and used a workshop to devise a new system for scheduling calls with varying frequencies, which led to far fewer wasted calls and improved relationships with the clients.

Visual–spatial intelligence
This involves images and spatial relationships.

Invite participants to draw, paint or colour to employ their visual–spatial intelligence. Ask them to design graphics, flowcharts or mazes to represent current or ideal systems with which they work.

Let them know that you'll be expecting them to swap seating positions with each other from time to time to keep visual intelligence stimulated by providing a change of perspective. (Of course, if someone has a strong preference for where they sit, let them stay put.)

Mindmapping – the gathering of information on a single page in graphic form – is useful for sorting ideas into order, note-taking, planning and recall.

I sometimes take photographs of significant moments during a course, which I send to participants as visual reminders of their learning. Another idea is to have a digital or Polaroid camera on hand for anyone to snap key moments instantaneously.

You can harness the spatial dimension to make learning points vivid. I recall a business strategy meeting in which each of us placed markers on the floor, using distances to represent 'how far we had to go' to achieve certain targets. We then walked the journeys slowly to stimulate ideas about the actions needed to enable us to reach each staging post. More sophisticated versions of this exercise use computer simulations to represent journeys which require greater precision.

The 'strategy walk' is an example of using a scale – a device for bringing many concepts to visual life. In the simple version, participants plot their current level of job satisfaction on a scale from 1–10 so that they can easily contrast their position with times past or future. I also use scales for appraisals and self-assessments, in which people rate how well they think that they grasp the course contents. This sort of activity requires a mixture of visual and mathematical intelligences.

For many people, visualizations are an effective way of calling on their visual-spatial intelligence to help achieve goals, clarify aims or remember important information.

At their most basic, visualizations consist simply of participants creating an image or series of images in their minds. Many will be doing this anyway. Some will do so if prompted, while others find it hard to generate any images. With the latter, it is worth persisting. The first time I was guided through a visualization, I saw virtually nothing in my 'mind's eye', certainly nothing of relevance and the process seemed a waste of time to me – although I appreciated that others were apparently 'getting the picture'. Next time, however, I was able to follow the journey with a great deal of detail and clarity and, to my utter amazement, the events I had generated in my mind occurred within the next few days – against heavy odds.

A guided visualization is when a speaker suggests a route or series of pictures for the visualizers. It may have more or less detail, depending on the purpose. You could design a 'journey' to help students memorize a safety sequence, a chemical process, a set of legal points or a first aid process. The example below – which you could use during a stress management programme – aims to help create images of a sanctuary which can be revisited at times of pressure.

This is a technique sometimes associated with self-hypnosis and is used by women preparing for childbirth, people in pain or those who want to give up smoking.

To put participants in a relaxed state, lower the lights, invite everyone to find a comfortable position – sitting or lying – and to breathe evenly, releasing tension from each part of their body in turn. As they relax, tell them they can shut their eyes and listen to the guided visualization – which may or may not conjure up images in their minds. Stress that there are no right or wrong ways to react to the process; whatever happens, happens. If they do 'see' things, they can make them as vivid and bright as possible, and note the details. Each visualization ends with a gentle reintroduction to the here and now, allowing time for participants to re-acclimatize themselves. Many people like to make a drawing of their sanctuary while the details are fresh.

ACTIVITY

Sanctuary visualization

Now you are relaxed, imagine you are setting out on a walk, a gentle but invigorating stroll. You are going to some places – either real or imaginary – that you like to visit. They may be actual places from your memory, or versions of them, or it may be that you find somewhere new, somewhere ideal. On the way, you first walk through a field in the countryside. The ground is firm and springy, and the air is fresh. Have a look at the scenery, notice the details.

You arrive at a place with water, perhaps a beach, a lake or a stream. Listen for the sounds, observe the water, feel the atmosphere.

And now you reach the place where you feel most comfortable, which has all the elements you need for this place, a place of your own, which is inspiring, safe, welcoming – a place that you can call your Sanctuary. Take in all the details, and notice how you feel about this place.

Visualizations are improvisational because the format leaves room for participants to make their own pictures. Each is personal, as you will find if you check descriptive details. If the purpose is to memorize a particular sequence, you would give more detail than in a visualization like Sanctuary, which aims to develop a resource in the form of mental strength and where more is therefore left to the individual imagination.

Kinaesthetic intelligence
This involves bodily awareness, involving manipulation of objects and physical skills.

It is the intelligence most developed in those who remember what is done, rather than said or seen. Their energy is rewardingly invested in touching, sculpting, modelling and in physical processes.

If we are teaching a physical skill, such as changing a tyre, passing a football or rewiring a fuse box, then the obvious route is for trainees to learn the skill by doing it.

Sometimes appealing to the kinaesthetic intelligence is best achieved by field trips, with opportunities for collecting items or scavenger hunts. Alternatively, trainees might make films, videos or tapes about the course contents. You can design physical games to make pertinent points about communication skills, and there is great scope for incorporating kinaesthetic intelligence into simulations and role-plays.

Even if there seems little scope for physical activity – in more academic or intellectual disciplines, for example – it is perilous to neglect this intelligence. At the very least, provide tactile stimulation for breaks. Bring a tempting array of juggling balls, marbles, cards, puzzles or books. Also, as part of your timetable of regular, frequent breaks, make sure that some include an element of exercise.

Educator Rudolph Arnheim recognized the importance of the kinaesthetic when he wrote:

> In our schools, reading, writing and arithmetic are practised as skills that detach the child from sensory (as opposed to verbal or mathematical) experience. . . Only in kindergarten. . . is education based on the co-operation of all the essential powers of the mind. Thereafter this natural and sensible procedure is dismissed as an obstacle to training in the proper kind of abstraction.

Paul E Dennison and colleagues developed a set of short, easily accomplished routines called 'Brain Gym' which revitalizes tiring participants. The exercises stimulate and harmonize both sides of the brain. One of the gentlest is writing with both hands at the same time, creating patterns mirrored along the central axis of the page. The sensation in the arms and fingers is akin to playing a keyboard. (Dennison, P E and Dennison, G E, 1988).

Musical intelligence
This intelligence is found in listening to music, playing instruments and singing.

We are probably all familiar with learning through music as children, with nursery rhymes and jingles. Similarly, we can appeal to the musical intelligence of trainees by using rhymes, songs, rhythms and raps. Either play your own, or invite participants to compose a rap, including all the day's key learning points, for performance to other members of the course.

Psychologist Georgi Lozanov and his followers have developed the use of active and passive 'concerts', in which review material is read aloud while learners listen to classical music of a certain tempo. This has proved particularly fruitful for memorizing foreign languages. Baroque music by Bach or Vivaldi for instance is ideal.

Having received and delivered short reviews of course material, while Baroque music played in the background at the regulation 60 beats per minute, I cannot personally confirm the learning efficacy of the method, but it certainly provided a pleasantly relaxing – and different – way of reflecting on key points towards the end of a day.

Interpersonal intelligence
This intelligence concerns understanding and interacting effectively with others.

Inspirational trainers display a command of interpersonal intelligence. They listen carefully, communicate well and know how to influence people. They react spontaneously and make people laugh. They are comfortable with giving and receiving feedback, negotiating, collaborating and, of course, teaching – whether as coach, mentor, facilitator or trainer. You make use of and develop interpersonal intelligence by encouraging participants to adopt these roles, giving each other feedback, for example, as part of some processes.

Many of the so-called 'soft skills', which involve different aspects of communication, are manifestations of interpersonal intelligence. As authoritarian styles within organizations go out of fashion, successful leaders and managers are increasingly those with highly-developed interpersonal skills, essentially displaying the ability to get on with a range of other people. Politicians, too, are finding that it pays to listen and communicate sensitively. Many training programmes teach interpersonal intelligence skills directly, and all live courses should include interpersonal work during some activities.

Intrapersonal intelligence
This intelligence refers to strengths in self-perception.

When people are skilled at planning and directing their own lives, they are displaying a strong intrapersonal intelligence. The inner world is the realm of this set of abilities, and it encompasses what author Daniel Goleman (1996) calls emotional intelligence.

Before learning about intrapersonal intelligence, I used to worry about course participants who stayed quiet and seemed rather unresponsive throughout the proceedings. I felt I should be doing more to 'jolly them along'. In fact, as their post-course feedback showed, they were mostly strongly reflective types, who gained just as much as others from the training, but in their own ways.

You can respect and encourage intrapersonal intelligence by allowing time for quiet, solitary reflection, during both preparation and review. Preparation might include 'thinking about what you already know about this subject'. A suitable review could be a self-assessment in which candidates reflect or score themselves on how well they have understood the topic.

Goal-setting – an intrapersonal activity *par excellence* – can also be presented in imaginative ways, such as allowing delegates to have three wishes.

INTELLIGENCE MIXTURES

Each trainee will possess individual strengths and weaknesses across the different intelligences. While traditional education has favoured the linguistic and mathematical-logical specialists, modern training needs to appeal to a broader band of capabilities.

Extremely able people visibly suffer during otherwise excellent lectures simply because they are made to listen for too long. They need physical activity to keep their brains alert, and as soon as the session involves any type of movement, they become vibrant contributors again.

A well designed training programme will include opportunities for participants to learn and shine through each intelligence. If your subject requires you to deliver a lecture, you could assign different roles to listeners – appointing scribes, illustrators, summarizers, reporters or even dramatists.

MORE WAYS TO KEEP TRAINING VIBRANT

Make use of contrast

It is clear that we need to provide variety in our programmes, partly to appeal to all learners and partly because each individual learner responds well to contrast. We gather information by perceiving contrasts. We notice something moving because something else is still. We perceive sound in relation to silence, loud to soft, fast to slow, tenseness to relaxation, and so on. Things have to differ to attract and keep our interest. A certain amount of sameness and predictability may be comfortable. Too much and we get bored.

Reveal the content early

Whatever the subject-matter, we can accelerate learning by making all the content available early in the course. Use wall posters, handouts, tapes and lectures to offer the material from different angles. You will deepen the understanding and experience of that content for all participants if you re-present the content through different processes.

Some trainers feel reluctant to reveal the content too early, preferring to parcel it out bit by bit. Their impulse to keep students alert for what is happening next is well founded, but they would achieve better results by making the processes the surprise rather than the material. Participants then benefit by learning through repetition without dullness and immediately reinforce their understanding of the material by putting it to use.

You can let participants know that they learn well by moving on before they feel they have mastered the current step. When they return to the material later, they will find it has now sunk in, or that they have surpassed the necessary level of skill in another way. My Suzuki-method piano teacher, for example, always starts me on the next, slightly harder, tune before I can play the current piece. This new fiendish difficulty soon makes the earlier work relatively easy.

Offer choices

If you offer choices, you encourage learners to be more receptive by increasing their feeling of being in control of their destiny. Improvisation is characterized by freedom within structure, and even if what must be learnt is fixed, you can find flexibility in the methods and processes. For example you can allow people the choice of working partners by varying the syndicate groups and giving them control over timing of breaks, choices of refreshment and music.

Participants appreciate a 'pass' option, so they can opt out of a round or an entire exercise if necessary (and because they can, they rarely do). If many pass, it is probably the wrong process at the wrong time, so either explain it more convincingly or drop it as quickly as possible and try something else. We can appreciate psychologist Carl Rogers' dictum in his book *Freedom to Learn*: 'The only learning that significantly influences behaviour is self-discovered, self-appropriated learning'.

Guard against information overload

When we are able to move confidently around the world of information, swapping expertise for anxiety, life feels easier, and we are in a position to learn more. Our trainees' attitudes to information, and the ways we make information available to them during our programmes, are critical.

Trainees will be in no mood to learn anything new if they feel they have too much information to handle. It is all too easy to allow them to become daunted or discouraged: if they cannot grasp it all, they may start to wonder whether to try at all. This means that we need ways of extending their sense of control over the information itself. A sheer glut of data will prove an unattractive prospect unless we can help them deal with it more effectively.

Richard Saul Wurman (1991) points out that a copy of the *New York Times* contains more information than the average person was likely to encounter in a lifetime in 17th-century England. He draws a distinction between data and information. Sometimes, there is too much data, and we need to filter it. Sometimes there are bits missing, and we may know what we want but not how to find it. 'Information is that which reduces uncertainty – which is the root cause of anxiety.'

Data becomes information only when it is meaningful. This means putting it into context or linking it to something we already know. As Reichian therapist Alexander Lowen puts it (1975: 62): 'Information does not become knowledge unless it has relevance to experience'. By experience he means doing or feeling – bodily. The mind plays a directive role, but learning is never entirely cerebral. 'Knowledge becomes understanding when it is coupled with feeling', adds Lowen, and we can apply this insight by ensuring that we offer a full sequence in training: presenting information, devising experiential process by which it can be turned into knowledge, and allowing time for reflection or further activities that synthesize knowledge into understanding, and understanding into knowledge. This approach helps avoid overload by breaking up information and channelling it towards different intelligences, in parallel.

We can also assist by teaching concepts rather than facts. Richard Saul Wurman (1991) suggests the most powerful learning is conceptual, with facts fitting into their context, connected to existing information. I encourage learners to illustrate my concepts with examples of their own. In this way, they put flesh on models for themselves and rapidly assimilate new ideas. A bonus is that they frequently suggest more telling illustrations than I would (or could). One delegate, when asked for an example of something which he could influence but which did not much concern him, suggested 'the life of ants which get in the way of my feet'.

Incorporate frequent breaks

Frequent breaks are important for keeping participants receptive to learning – one per hour is a good rough guide. Studies show that we tend to remember the first and last things in any session, and the simple logic is that more breaks mean more 'firsts and lasts', which means more is recalled.

A good guideline is to switch disciplines at twenty-minute segments within the hour, to keep boredom at bay and to exploit this recall effect. Trust participants to tell you if they are growing restless and allow them to call for a change of activity or time-out.

Allow learners to follow their own question trails

We acquire and remember new knowledge only if it stimulates our curiosity. Interest precedes learning, and the strongest signals of interest and curiosity are questions. When trainers overcome any fear of being questioned – by realizing that they need not personally have all the answers – they can create the conditions in which trainees construct their own information trails routed by the questions they ask.

Many of us feel that we need some kind of licence to ask questions. When I was a journalist, I could use my occupational persona to ask questions. The nature of the job meant that it was acceptable to be direct, probing, even cheeky or rude. Many professions allow their members to ask questions in their particular fields. In their personae, doctors ask about health, counsellors about feelings, students about their subjects, police and lawyers about suspicious behaviour.

Inspirational trainers issue their participants a licence to ask whatever questions they want. Tell them that they can. Have a slogan on the wall: 'There are no stupid questions, only stupid answers'. Welcome questions when they are asked.

Encurige mistikes

When Edwin Land was inventing instant film, he described his attempts as trying to use an impossible chemistry and a non-existent technology to make an unmanufacturable product for which there was no discernible demand. This, he felt, created the optimum working conditions.

Ed Moses, the world champion hurdler, said, 'I lost a lot in high school and college. Maybe as often as I won. I just didn't think about it in terms of losing. I was preparing.'

Success and failure are largely questions of perspective. Sometimes it takes magnificent failure to create the conditions for ultimate success. Sometimes it is pure accident that brings the breakthrough.

We live in a society where mistakes and 'failure' are highlighted and frowned upon. One way to stop blaming ourselves and others is to appreciate that if one thing leads to another, we can simply consider it an outcome. Many organizations find this an attitude worth cultivating amongst their workers. In any creative environment it is crucial. As writer Cynthia Heimel recommends, 'When in doubt, make a fool of yourself. There is a microscopically thin line between being brilliantly creative and acting like the most gigantic idiot on earth. So what the hell, leap'. And remember, a training programme is a creative environment – at least it is if we want it to be a place of discovery, change and learning.

As the learning process is not always continuous, providing a steady stream of facts may not be the best way to create learning conditions. If you encourage experiment, your trainees will enjoy moments of learning, characterized by feelings of sudden insight, 'clicking' and 'gelling'.

Attend to group spirit

By keeping a group in good spirits, more often than not you will carry doubters and pessimists through moments which might otherwise have them protesting or engaging in futile argument. It is difficult to maintain a mood contrary to all those around you. Once you have created conditions conducive to learning, all you need do is maintain them.

A group's needs are defined by the course objectives – to which group members may well have contributed. I attended one seminar where there seemed to be confusion about objectives: about half of us had come to discuss learning organizations, and the others had come to start one. The facilitator failed to clarify the ambiguity and even encouraged us to seek fulfilment of any 'deeper' objectives we had not yet expressed! By the final session of the day there was open conflict, and the facilitator was prevented from leading his planned discussion about large learning organizations (which half of us were eagerly anticipating) and we spent the time developing our on-the-spot learning organization by way of holding hands, swaying and humming. I expect we all learnt something. . .

When a group is learning, the spirit tends to be good, so if the atmosphere of a session seems to be faltering, it is time to consider whether anyone is learning anything useful. If the answer is doubtful, you could switch to a part of the programme about which you are more confident that participants will gain information, wisdom or insight. Your repertoire will include some reliable processes, which invariably lead to good learning and positive moods. Use them at strategic intervals to keep the spirit on track.

Use humour

Humour is an attractive emotional gateway to education. Research shows that putting people in a good mood, for example by telling them jokes, helps them think through problems with more ingenuity. While stress inhibits learning, humour is a tremendous way of relieving tension and opening the doors to memory and understanding.

Inspirational trainers can develop two particular strands of humour. One is to seek wit and paradox to illuminate material from unusual angles, perhaps in the form of quotations. For a presentation skills course, for example, there's Sir George Jessel's epigram: 'The human brain starts working the moment you are born and never stops until you stand up to speak in public'. The other is the more 'situational' skill of capitalizing on opportunities to make the group laugh – perhaps through making light of difficulties. One example of this occurred during a four-day course for therapists. Most of the material was about one-to-one interviewing, and there were several requests for information about group work. Eventually the trainer found a videotape of a session with a group of clients. Unfortunately the sound quality was so poor, with such overwhelming background noise, that the interview was inaudible. The trainer apologized, switched the tape off after about 30 seconds and said, 'There we are: that's group work'.

119

MAKING WORK MORE LIKE PLAY

The application of these creative principles makes learning more like play. When training is great fun, the more puritan participants guiltily worry that it is not real work. Reassure them that the playful elements indicate that more is being achieved, and that they might explore ways of occasionally making their own work more like play. If that fails, simply apologize for the laughter.

Play can be taken lightly, but also – as it becomes absorbing – as seriously as we like. With play we have the feeling of free choice. We could be doing something else, but have made the decision to play. Traditional work structures offer less freedom in this respect, but more recent trends – from flexi-time to self-employment in the arena of one's hobbies and in working from home – blur the distinctions.

Build the features of play into training programmes and, as participants thrive on the opportunity to express themselves and use their talents, they may even opt to take new arrangements and attitudes back with them into their working life.

INSPIRATIONS

- Vary your style and pace to accommodate different learners' preferences. People are different: anthropologist Clyde Kluckhohn stated it succinctly: 'Every man is like every other man, like some other men, like no other man'.
- Give the big picture first.
- Use colour and music to enrich the learning environment.
- Deploy multiple intelligences to engage and inspire you and your participants.
- Make work more like play: encourage mistakes and a 'have-a-go' attitude, then everyone will learn more.

8

Energize!

Controlling energy is an exciting and subtle way of helping participants ride the waves of inspiration. To do so skilfully we need sufficient energy available to us, with the ability to access and channel it in whichever directions we choose.

People learn more when they are feeling alert, less when tired. As trainers we can help them to maintain optimum receptivity levels. When we understand and use energy wisely, we support ourselves too.

The keys to energy are: awareness – being able to sense its flow around a group; and knowing how to shift energy in the most helpful directions. Sometimes it is important to quieten and calm a group. More often, it is useful to raise energy levels.

In old-style lecture sessions energy is suppressed because trainees spend too long sitting down immobile. They are restricted in terms of breathing and movement, and are probably given too few breaks. Surplus energy begins to leak out in the form of fidgeting and side-shows, such as doodling and whispering. Listeners may reduce energy output and slump or even sleep. The two antidotes which can be incorporated even when there is going to be a huge amount of lecture material are frequent breaks and a plentiful supply of fresh air.

What more can we do? And how can we use energy awareness to enhance course content when we don't want to interrupt our flow with a break?

ENERGY RAISERS

If we feel that the level of energy in the room is too low – which is confirmed by the sight of people yawning or shifting uncomfortably in their seats – we can do something about it.

Some groups are surprised when I propose a physical activity. They are not used to this and seem to imagine that their intellectual presence is enough – they are here in mind but not body. I stress that, despite any superficial resemblance to PE at school, it won't be too demanding: there is an opt-out clause, and they will feel immediate learning benefits.

The following physical activities can be used as session ice-breakers or as intelligent ways to raise energy at any time during a programme.

Earth, air, fire, water

This is an elementary warm-up, a short, comprehensive routine for putting us in a good condition to learn.

ACTIVITY

Elemental warm-up

Tell the group that we are going to prepare ourselves completely for the activities ahead and that we shall do so according to accepted medieval practice, dating from the International Conference of the Dark Ages circa 1142. (This perspective is especially appreciated when we are working with a hi-tech company or anyone medical.)

Begin with 'Air' in the form of deep breathing. Everybody stands up and breathes deeply, allowing oxygen to raise their energy. Ask the participants to imagine the whole body as a lung, capable of breathing then expelling the air all the way into and out from our fingers and toes.

Participants may benefit from you naming the parts along an imagined oxygen route – hearing it 'pass into your chest, shoulders, along your upper arms, elbows and out through your hands right into your fingers; up into your face and onto your scalp; into your stomach, pelvis, thighs and knees, through your legs, ankles and feet and right out into your toes'. This makes the exercise more tangible (if less scientific).

Alternatively, encourage everyone to yawn, first by faking a few deep yawns, accompanied by a full arm-raising stretch, then allowing any real yawns to emerge. Yawning is our best way of quickly compensating for a shortage of oxygen. When delivering a content-heavy course, which could be in danger of being a little stifling at times, announce that yawns will be taken as a sign of appreciation. Deliberate yawns generally work well to start early-morning sessions.

continued on page 123

'Earth' consists of making a connection to the floor. We speak of feeling 'grounded'. This part of the activity returns to the source of the metaphor and makes it literal.

ACTIVITY

Join in with the participants in vigorous stepping, stamping and jumping. Get everyone to rub their feet against the floor (without shoes if there is no danger of embarrassment or splinters), stretching the foot and noticing the contact of all sides of the triangle - that is, the inside and outside of the foot from the heel and the line of the toes. The aim is to gain awareness of our feet, of their connection with the floor, which results in a feeling of greater stability and security throughout our bodies.

continued below

The Earth exercise benefits anyone who suffers from nervousness before presentations, especially if the nerves manifest themselves as 'wobbliness', 'shaking' or the like. Such people feel themselves steadied and much more secure. They notice immediate improvements in their voice projection, and the audience will see them as stiller and more convincing.

ACTIVITY

For 'Fire' we move – sharp, jagged, pointing and flashing arms and legs, bony, moving as if in a wild dance. You might say, 'Hey, we're at a rave' (or disco, depending on the age of the group). Ask everyone to feel the energy charge to their extremities; imagine that we are fiery, blazing presences.

continued on page 124

This exercise can spectacularly raise the energy levels of subdued, placid types who may be reluctant to leave their normal, comfortable state, and will satisfy themselves with a token spark or two unless they find themselves carried along by the impetus of the group.

As the lightness of air contrasts with the heaviness of earth, so the flickering of fire contrasts with the graceful flow of water.

ACTIVITY

Suggest moving with classic elegance, gliding, rotating wrists, arms, ankles, then streaming to another part of the room, as if the participants and their surroundings are all water. This is like Tai Chi or 'Eurythmy', the dance movement taught in Rudolf Steiner schools.

continued below

The process ends by finding balance. We achieve balance by recalling each of the elements and harmonizing them.

ACTIVITY

Ask everyone to notice how the elements feel in their bodies now – which is dominant, which weakest. Point out that they can consciously adjust the balance between the elements. We can control our mix into whatever interplay is needed. To make the right combination now, ask people to review the four parts of the activity in quick succession, to tap into each element again. The review also serves to fix the learning into memory.

Different participants can gain more from different elements, depending on their current strengths and weaknesses. Tell them the Greek myth of Hercules, who fought with Antaeus, knocking him down repeatedly, but still seemed to be losing the fight. Suddenly he realized that Antaeus was the son of Mother Earth, and drew strength each time he touched the ground. Hercules then lifted Antaeus and held him in the air until he was defeated.

Go outdoors

One of the most effective ways of moderating energy is to take a group outside. If the weather is reasonable, it creates a memorable session and raises the energy through better breathing. Energy is also affected by horizons. One of the reasons we seek spectacular views and enjoy seascapes is the energy which we derive from the command of the view. For the moment we may feel like monarchs – useful as an antidote to feelings of helplessness which may, for instance, have been expressed by a group working under intense pressure or battling with change.

It is especially beneficial to go outdoors – perhaps for discussions in pairs – if the room lacks lighting or if sound quality is muffled. Lungs, eyes, ears and spirit – and therefore learning – all respond well to the change.

Find balance

We can find balance in an immediate physical sense too. Whenever self-consciousness and composure are at issue – in presentation skills sessions and risk-taking, for example – the next exercise prepares trainees for the appropriate learning.

ACTIVITY

Balance

Ask everyone to stand on one foot, and swivel and stretch to the limits of their balance. The instruction is to keep twisting and extending – slowly and carefully – to find the points where you overbalance and need to fall over or support yourself with a hand or the other foot. Then try the other foot. Note which foot affords more stability.

There's often much laughter as people extend themselves in unfamiliar swan-like poses. Ask them to take note of how far they are stretching, as a benchmark for another attempt later.

Next introduce a greater degree of precision. Ask the participants to cradle one knee with both hands and to lift the knee a little higher, but without forcing the leg to go further than is comfortable. Next, ask them to release the hands, keeping the knee where it is and stretch the arms out wide. The idea is to contemplate and preferably maintain balance in this position. Some people may topple, as it can be quite a tricky pose. Repeat the sequence with the other leg.

THE ALEXANDER TECHNIQUE

So far, the balance exercises have given us experiences of poise and toppling, a chance to experiment and note how our balancing feels. We may have tipped over at certain points, or have impressed ourselves by the lengths we can stretch while still maintaining our bodies with minimal support.

We can borrow some concepts and practices from the Alexander Technique – a one-to-one therapy designed by Australian actor F M Alexander and practised throughout the world – to learn how to improve and develop our balance. About half the participants in any group experience an immediate improvement in their physical (and thus their whole) use and are interested to find out more. The others, while missing the thrill of discovery, do at least have a good stretch.

The Alexander Technique is particularly appropriate for relearning skills in situations where trainees are tempted to continue doing the same things in the same ways as before. It is a habit-breaker.

By helping us gain awareness of ourselves in the present, these processes encourage us to attend to what we are doing and how we are doing it. We can engender a state of 'here and now', a condition in which we are attentive, present, ready, poised and so at our best for noticing, absorbing and making choices. We benefit from stopping and settling ourselves, if only to avoid falling into the trap of following an old, habitual pattern which, because it is practised and familiar, cannot by its nature be improvised.

To learn something implies doing it differently. If we are in the grip of habit, we need to unlearn what we usually do. In the Alexander Technique – and this will be a familiar refrain for most trainers – the next thing is often to not do the thing we usually do.

Stop

If you want to make the ideas of stopping and unlearning explicit, continue the balance sequence by repeating the two exercises, after suggesting to participants that:

- they are to stop and pause for a brief moment before each step of the sequence;
- they allow their head to lead them in all the movements;
- they notice the differences that the first two actions make to the quality of their movement, to the balance they feel, and to the distances that they can now stretch with the same – or less – degree of effort.

Most of us are unused to allowing our head to lead us in movement. Allowing is significantly different from thrusting, pulling or stretching. We are in the domain of thought rather than physical effort. A helpful image which you can suggest to the group is that of our head as a helium balloon, attached to the piece of string that is our neck. The balloon rises gently because it is light, but cannot hurt the string, which follows every movement – however delicate – of the leading balloon.

Typically participants will experience a greater flexibility and range of movement. Some will really surprise themselves with the difference that 'stopping' and 'allowing' make.

If you realize that you are doing something inefficiently, stopping creates space, room and opportunity to replace the old use with a new and improved way. The practice of 'Stop', then, can be called upon whenever a participant equates the trouble with doing something new as 'I can't seem to let go of the old way of doing this'.

You can probably think of many applications for 'Stop' in your training programmes, particularly if they involve the management of change. When I have divided participants into teams to generate new sets of applications for 'Stop' in their own areas of expertise, they have made suggestions ranging from 'Stop the lunacy' of some ancient practice ('Stop clocking on', for example, as we entrust timekeeping to the workers) to 'Stop the New Scheme' – because it hasn't been market-tested yet. So much of what happens in organizations is driven by inertia, and 'Stop' can put the brakes on runaway practices.

Of course, in the free moment that 'Stop' provides, we have an instant in which we can choose to follow the path that we have traditionally followed. If it still seems like a good idea, at least we know we are not doing so automatically.

Hand to hand

The following activity continues the theme of balance.

ACTIVITY

Tip to tip

Ask the participants to close their eyes and very slowly move their open hands together, so that right fingertips meet left. They are to approach so slowly that any warmth or energy from the hands is felt before they actually touch. Ask them to note, without self-consciousness or self-criticism, if fingers meet tip to tip as expected, or if their perception of where their hands are is different from the reality. Repeat the process to discover whether everyone has learnt anything – such as an increased awareness of where their hands are in space.

USING LESS EFFORT

Prophetic novelist and writer Aldous Huxley formulated a Law of Reversed Effort, which proposed: 'The harder we try with the conscious will to do something, the less we shall succeed. Proficiency and the results of proficiency come only to those who have learnt the paradoxical art of doing and not doing'. Learning often takes place when we are not concentrating directly on the object of the learning. There are at least three facets to this paradox.

The first concerns levels of concentration. If concentration equals effort, then it can be counterproductive. Everyone is familiar with tasks where 'the harder you try, the harder it gets'. Yet sometimes it is not enough simply to know this. We need ways to help us try less hard.

This is where the second facet proves useful. Learning often takes place 'next to' or 'below the surface of' an activity. Setting tasks with a certain amount of misdirection or switching of attention exploits this ability. For example, if the purpose is to learn how we operate in a team, we can encourage participants to concentrate on making a product, winning a contest or some other complex activity. Their primary attention is on this task, rather than on the objective of teambuilding.

In the review at the end of the exercise, we can direct participants to consider how they performed as team players. Although, during the activity, this aspect engaged only their peripheral attention, they will easily be able to reflect on the team aspects of their experience and learn from it.

The third facet is that there are times when we achieve more by directing our efforts towards not doing something wrong than striving to do something right. In a communications exercise, the instruction 'Please do not interrupt or speak until the other person indicates they have finished' can open a door to attentive listening in a way that asking 'Listen attentively' cannot. Trying directly to get something right sometimes makes us struggle, strain and set ourselves up to fail.

DOING WITHOUT NAMING

In the exercises described earlier, we might also note that we have improved our balance by *doing* something. By doing something physically new, learning has not taken place purely in the head but also in the muscles; this will remain in the body for as long as we continue.

This mind-body combination is powerful. If you only read about a process, you learn less than if you try it for yourself. Understanding is enhanced by doing. To understand the balance sequence fully as a training exercise, you would need to go through the process with a training group. At that point it becomes your own, and you are in a position to employ it in new, creative ways.

Some of the concepts I describe derive from drama. Others are from Accelerated Learning, NLP and from sports training (both psychological and physical), all areas rich in ideas for application in our work as trainers.

To make the applications as valuable as possible, be wary of accepting all of the vocabulary that accompanies the discipline. NLP, for example, defines concepts such as 'mirroring', 'pacing' and 'reframing', to create a particular understanding of experience. There's an advantage in such a system in that it offers practitioners a sense of security: things are defined just so; we will tend to find the connections the system tells us to look for. A potential disadvantage is that we could miss some of the organic ways in which our experience orders itself.

As a trainer concerned with allowing each learner to validate their own experience, I feel an affinity with disciplines such as the Alexander Technique and Feldenkrais, which explicitly align themselves with organic notions of order – in particular our skeletal structure. These seem to carry with them less sense of an outside authority residing in a practitioner (although just such authority may suit some trainers in some circumstances).

Ruthy Alon develops the work of physical pioneer Moshe Feldenkrais in her fascinating book *Mindful Spontaneity* (1996), and observes that there is no such thing as boundless freedom. We always operate within structures, within which we are free to relate appropriately or inappropriately. The Feldenkrais limits are gravity and our bones. Although it may sound paradoxical, Alon expounds a grammar of spontaneity. The grammar is revealed through a series of experiments which each isolate a physical movement; you aim to become aware of how you are affected by small changes in the way you accomplish that movement.

One of the best reasons for using movement in inspirational training is to allow people to experience emotional states without vulnerability. The exercises are not about emotion. We simply recognize that emotions are likely to arise during them, that they can be noted, examined clearly and used to widen our range of options. When we are ready to accept whatever emotions shift during an experience, we are closer to allowing it to be a learning experience. We know that people learn more when they are less anxious. By accepting emotion, we reduce anxiety. The learner is free to move beyond the 'stuck' state that inhibits progress.

These are therapeutic ideas, having much in common with Alexander Lowen, Wilhelm Reich and the dramatherapy school of Moreno and, while training is not therapy, it can certainly borrow usefully from both 'physical' and 'talk' therapies.

In my opinion, the most effective training is holistic. When trainees are treated as complete beings, with their own individual aspirations, abilities and ways of understanding, we can avoid the reductionist tendencies that mar so many training initiatives.

HEAD, HEART AND GUTS

An effective way of ensuring a holistic approach is to direct your training simultaneously at three levels: head, heart and guts.

Head

Training must make sense in a logical and ordered way. We study and learn because it will help us to achieve rational objectives. Training has helped countless others to do so in the past, and we can offer reasons to account for this. Educators and trainers have refined and improved the process over the years and, if anyone finds ways of doing things better, rational trainers will listen to the reasons, assess them and change their methods accordingly.

Training techniques that appeal particularly to the intellectual level include conceptual models, closely reasoned lectures, flowcharts, puzzles, quizzes and demonstrations of how things work.

Heart

Unlike cold logic, the heart level requires emotion, warmth and empathy. The training experience should be pleasurable. The best trainers communicate humanity, and participants will become a cohesive group rather than isolated individuals.

Heartfelt laughter is a good sign that training is working at the emotional level. When the accelerated learning instructor Paul Scheele subtly led an audience into holding hands – accomplishing a positive emotional bonding – he released what could have been an awkward and counterproductive tension by saying, 'We don't all have to sing *Kum By Ya* now, do we?'.

Processes which involve recall of doing things successfully – the photograph introduction activity and many teambuilding exercises, for instance – operate primarily on the emotional level.

Guts

The third level is visceral and concerns deep, almost primitive, learning. It is an intuitive experience of learning, that gut feeling which tells us that, without change, we are in danger. It is learning which connects to motivation by way of our deepest wishes or strongest fears.

Processes which tap into sheer excitement or profound relaxation, visualizations which take us on inner journeys that can touch the soul and exercises of intuition are ways of reaching and affecting participants at this level. Many processes have this potential at times. It is never possible to be sure just what impression activities are having on each participant. We do not need to know, so long as we are aware of the sorts of impacts that our work is likely to have. Within that loose framework, some processes are clearly more intellectual, while others are more affective.

Although I have described this level as 'deep', I do not intend that as 'better' or even 'more meaningful'; it is deep rather in the sense of involving the 'reptilian brain' we have in common with our oldest evolutionary ancestors.

For training to hit home, it must touch each of these levels at least some of the time. The most powerful parts will be those that combine two or all three at once. Outdoor training, with obvious elements of danger, clearly operates partly at the visceral level. It may be weaker at the level of intellect – the challenges of white-water canoeing do not readily parallel the intricate use of an appraisal interview to motivate a sales manager – but each has its place.

Contrary to popular belief, heart and intellect are not mutually exclusive. Head, heart and guts combine to create holistic experiences which have far more profound impacts than any element in isolation.

EBB AND FLOW

Energy ebbs and flows, and it would be a mistake to expect everyone to maintain high energy all the way through a programme. A mix of activities allows for dynamic sections balanced with more reflective interludes.

As well as energizers, inspirational trainers need a pack of calmers. These include:

- reflections;
- reviews;
- reading individually;
- writing individually;
- meditations;
- visualizations;
- calming exercises – borrowed from yoga, Tai Chi or similar disciplines.

Energy charts

Trainers begin to master a group's energy pattern by gaining an awareness of their own. Recognize when you feel galvanized and when you need rests. If your patterns are broadly similar to the group's, it is easier to call on your reserves to enthuse convincingly when you need to generate energy, and not feel you are buzzing wastefully when others need to step back and take stock.

When we ask participants on Train The Trainer courses to monitor the rise and fall of their energy through a day, we see something like the results in Figure 8.1.

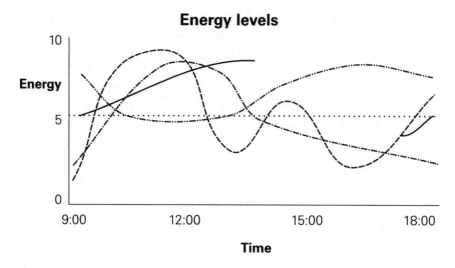

Figure 8.1 *Energy levels*

Although each participant traces a unique pattern, certain trends are generally clear. For example, there is often an energy slump as people digest their meal. Trainers refer to the session after lunch as the graveyard shift, because it is so difficult to discern signs of life.

One option is to accept that certain sessions are likely to be low on energy and, rather than try to fight it, use such processes as writing, multiple choice form-filling or paired discussions about an easily accessible subject. Alternatively, realize that we shall need to pump in plenty of vigour to get some people moving, if that's what you want at this time. Another solution is to arrange a light lunch of healthy foods, encourage a brisk walk between lunch and the first afternoon session, trust that nobody has a secret cache of chocolate, and so avoid the usual energy-draining torpor.

If we are training people in health-related matters, and have a holistic or medical thrust to our content, it seems fair to back the messages of the programme by providing food that supports what we know about good diet and nutrition. This can also apply to programmes about stress and time management. Perhaps volunteers could experiment with caffeine-free days, for example, and note the impact on their energy charts.

TRAINERS' ENERGY

Sometimes we, as trainers, slip into a rut, particularly if we have to run the same course over and over again, or when we are stuck with the same group for months (or years) at a time. Training days may seem too long because the client is demanding too much too quickly. We never seem to have the time for a break to refresh ourselves.

These are recipes for personal and professional disaster. If the work grows too onerous or dull, you are in danger of running down and staying that way. And your effectiveness will diminish – largely because you have less energy to invest, your delivery is duller and everything inevitably comes across to the recipients as stale.

When whole sectors of professionals find themselves in that position – such as British school-teachers at the start of this century (arguably) – the impact is far-reaching, because the status of that profession is then at risk. If the quality of work is questioned, and the professionals concerned lack the time or energy to improve their position, their collective reputation is damaged, the profession is less attractive to new recruits, and drastic measures may be needed.

Trainers must look after themselves. If you are in a department where colleagues also run programmes, arrange to swap courses from time to time. Perhaps you can find ways of changing places mid-course – turning solo shows into double-acts, bringing new dynamics into play, so that you both get a new perspective (as do your participants).

Arrange time for devising as well as delivering. They are two separate, contrasting activities and they feed well off each other.

■NSPIRATIONS

Training for trainers

Go on training courses where you will experience inspirational training for yourself. Find out what others are doing well. Steal ideas, borrow activities. Inspire yourself to develop new twists on your own routines from your observation of others.

In the space of a few months, I enjoyed private piano coaching, a four-day event on solution-focused strategies, and a one-day seminar about building a learning organization. All made tangible differences to my own projects.

You are already showing an interest in breaking out of any insularity by considering the material in this book. If you use it to inspire yourself to take actions, then booking a course – in any subject you fancy – will prove an effective step in personal development. The content of the course will have its own appeal, and you will also be aware of the processes the trainer uses. Any trainer going on a course therefore gets double value.

When you find more energy available to you, you will immediately start expressing it in the delivery of training. It will seem easier to pump energy into a room at key moments to lift a group, perhaps to get them to follow an instruction. In the film *Dead Poets Society*, Robin Williams plays a teacher facing a reluctant class which could quite easily refuse to obey him. In fact the first time he wants the class to change position and gather round him, he says 'Huddle down!' and nothing happens. He gets them to obey by sheer force of energy: a louder, more persuasive 'Huddle round!' And so they move.

One trainer described that style as 'bullying', although her eight colleagues disagreed. Clearly, one person's bullying is another's strong encouragement. The important point was for her to find her own way of using that degree of energy to achieve the same result without bullying. After more thought, she decided she would manage that situation by saying, 'Huddle round – please!'.

Enthusiasm

If you convey enthusiasm for your subject, you will appeal to almost any audience. They sense your excitement and will want to participate in it. Because enthusiasm is such a well-known way of connecting, it has become tarnished by association with people whom we don't necessarily want to hear from – for example, unwanted salespeople pitching all manner of products, services and beliefs which we might prefer to avoid. Yet enthusiasm, if genuine and appropriate, is a building-block for charisma – that ability of a speaker or presenter to lead through personal presence.

MIXING METAPHORS

Any trainer will have fields of expertise other than standard training practice and can add value by finding bridges between those disciplines and the area of instruction. One way is to devise activities and share insights based on one and appropriate to the other.

Inspirational training encourages you to dip into different practices, taking the elements which work for you and your trainees and producing your own distinctive mix. By experimenting, you and your participants will make new connections and discover excellent aids to training and development.

NLP founders Richard Bandler and John Grinder (1990:74) wrote: 'I think you have an obligation to experiment with every client to make yourself more skilled, because in the long run you are going to be able to help more people more expediently. If, under the guise of professionalism, you don't try to expand your skills and experiment, basically I think you are missing the point and professionalism becomes just one way to limit yourself'.

Any exciting mixture of processes will generate the energy you need for influencing group response. By deliberately varying energy outlay, you will change pace and create contrasts, switching from animation to calmness to a sense of buzz, excitement and 'action-about-to-happen'. You can exude stillness, control and calm, or create a sense of intensity, importance and anticipation. The proper deployment of energy is the fuel of the inspirational learning session.

NSPIRATIONS

- Stay aware of your own energy and that of the group.
- Introduce a variety of physical processes.
- Go outdoors.
- You can calm a group as well as raise their energy.
- It often pays to 'stop' before moving on.
- Attend other trainers' courses to keep yourself up to date.

9

Resources from participants

By drawing on the experience and skills of the group, the trainer taps into a prime and often underrated resource.

As emphasis passes from one-dimensional lecture-driven content-heavy courses towards process-rich inspirational learning, one of the principal changes will be our appreciation that the group is a prime resource. Instead of being recipients of our wisdom, trainees become active participants. This goes beyond the accelerated learning concept that they can learn faster and remember more. And it means more than merely 'joining in' with games and exercises.

Inspirational training pre-supposes a multidimensional pattern in which participants will help provide content, contribute to the agenda and join in with research towards their own development. It is a method reminiscent of 'Active Birth', where the woman takes control of her own childbirth experience, assisted by supportive attendants.

STARTING FROM WHERE WE ARE

The group contains experience and skills. Our task is to discover the nature and extent of this resource, work out how it is pertinent and create a context in which to harness it for the benefit of all.

Let's suppose that we know the purpose of the programme and have a rough idea of the content we would like to deliver. Instead of telling the group exactly what they are going to learn, the trainer begins by finding out what the participants already know, or, in the case of skills, what they can already do.

This approach has the potential to save a huge amount of time and effort as we can avoid covering old ground and instead head straight for the exciting and uncharted terrain of 'unconscious competence', switching back and forth from there to conscious competence as we make knowledge and skill explicit. Acknowledging existing skills and promising efficient use of delegates' time creates goodwill too.

Our aim, therefore, is to use the participants' current position as a starting point. We might help them realize just how much they know, we might illuminate from new angles, but essentially we want to build on existing knowledge and abilities. My father-in-law, a professional cartoonist and talented teacher, used to say that when he was a child in art class he found himself agreeing with everything his teacher told him. On some intuitive level he felt he 'knew' what was coming next. By building on our group's existing expertise, we immediately make learning easier for them – an experience which feels 'right'.

This chimes with theories of learning which suggest that new information needs to be attached to existing knowledge, through connections that make sense. We can then tackle conscious incompetence – the area where the learner is aware of a shortfall – with confidence and strength.

We therefore need appropriate ways of finding out what's already known, so we might:

- devise a questionnaire;
- ask individuals to draw a mindmap of their current knowledge;
- ask the group to construct a mindmap jointly;
- solicit demonstrations of the current levels of competence in individuals or the group.

For an adult education history class, for example, a short, light-hearted quiz would establish the level of knowledge.

An informal discussion about a session subject reveals who knows what, who knows more than most and the general attitude to the subject. If you want to assess experience, you could ask each person to describe what they have done so far. This is a good technique when you will be working with them over a period of days or longer, or when everyone can keep their experience brief: 'I've completed two half-hour scripts so far, both of which have been swiftly returned by the BBC drama department with a polite note'.

Another method is to ask small groups to present what they know either verbally or with a flipchart or as a mindmap. This works well when there are too many people to listen to individually and if their depth of knowledge is likely to be reasonably uniform.

ACTIVITY

Stand up: show what you know

If your subject is a demonstrable, practical skill, organize an exercise for participants to show their current competence. Near the beginning of courses on making presentations, for example, I ask them in turn to describe their objectives. When the round is complete, I indicate that everyone has made a short, spontaneous presentation. In this way, they demonstrate their current ability to themselves as well as to the trainer.

In a course for stand-up comedians, I ask each performer to speak for a couple of minutes on stage. This usually reveals a fund of promising topics for their material, as well as revealing their specific needs in terms of tutoring in basic stage skills.

BRINGING FEAR AND PHOTOS

Begin the process of encouraging trainees to harness their own resources even before a training event starts, by asking them to bring items to the course. This generates immediate mental, physical and emotional involvement, if the items requested are sufficiently resonant, and helps the trainer bring the emotional currents to the surface. This is especially important when dealing with change or uncertainty, when participants are likely to be frightened about fundamental aspects of their lives – for example, the future of their jobs and the potential consequences for family life, homes and status. They will need to access their emotional resources if useful learning is to occur.

Until the fears – even if mild – are acknowledged, they will be a barrier to learning. If people's concerns are validated, the underlying fears may remain but they no longer need block the way forward. It is as if they have been temporarily suspended. If we can deal with fears constructively, we may even be able to transform the underlying emotion to one of hope.

Often participants prefer to avoid mentioning their concerns and are unlikely to welcome any head-on approach from a trainer they hardly know. In many corporate cultures – as in public schools, sports clubs and other male-dominated institutions – fear is either suppressed or ignored. The favoured emotions are the macho set of bravado, aggression, competition. These tough, progressive qualities leave little room for doubt, fear or sensitivity.

The Photos game

The Photos game provides a resource-based, unthreateningly tangential way to allow the expression of emotions. It also serves as a pre-course appetizer and initiative indicator.

The game worked well, for example, in a course called Managing Uncertainty, a series of workshops designed to equip participants to deal with far-reaching changes in their workplaces. In this situation, it was clearly useful for trainees to know how they and their colleagues tended to handle uncertainty. By analysing reactions, they could check how well their responses were serving them, and whether they might benefit by making adjustments.

ACTIVITY

Three photographs

In the joining instructions, ask participants to bring three photographs to the course. Give no other information about the photos – no hint of how they are to be used, or how to select them, who should have taken them or what they might be photos of.

continued on page 140

The reactions are fascinating – indicating a range of responses from intellectual stimulation and inventively resourceful solutions to the challenge, to fear and even apathy. Some feel so threatened by even this playful level of uncertainty that they bring along no photos at all. From a group of eight production supervisors in a Ford factory, for example, only one brought three photographs into the room – two others said they had them in their cars, in case they really needed them. As we shall see, even this no-show reaction serves a purpose.

The Ford group claimed that they were so stressed and busy that they hadn't had time, within their priorities, to select any photos. It also transpired that this particular group only worked beyond their precisely specified duties within the factory if written memos were followed up by a personal call, or if the person asking was unusually senior. This proved to be a key discovery for implementing effective change later.

Many people ring up in advance of a course to try to find out more. These tend to be the well-organized types who dislike uncertainty and are willing to do something practical about it. Others hedge their bets for as long as possible by bringing a wide selection of photos, hoping to narrow the choice at the last moment when they have more information.

ACTIVITY

During the session, ask people what they think the photos are for.

continued on page 141

Guesses generally include 'psychological testing', 'to find out what's most important to us' and 'for using in a collage'. Quite a few participants ask cautiously if the photos are going to be damaged – their images are understandably precious.

In fact the game is to help people appreciate how they reacted to the uncertainty, to note what steps they took and how they feel at each successive stage, as they find out that they are actually to introduce themselves to the other participants, using their photos as prompts or subject headings if they wish.

It was illuminating for the Ford personnel to realize that what they deemed unimportant from their perspective might be something important to the person asking. This, incidentally, is a helpful insight for anyone wishing to become a skilled negotiator, as one of the arts is to trade things which seem more valuable to your counterpart than they do to you.

In the Photos game, the uncertainty becomes a certainty. Those who feared unpleasant psychological probing feel a sense of relief. Those who brought photos that readily illustrate their lives feel vindicated, and everyone realizes that in this instance there was no such thing as a wrong reaction to uncertainty.

What is noticeable is that the photos are resource icons, often illustrating important people, places and events in participants' lives, and that they put the current uncertainties of the workplace into perspective. Their evocative qualities remind people of happy times, sustaining relationships and away-from-work interests. The pictures are powerful generators of positive emotions.

ACTIVITY ─────────────────────────────────

Participants' reactions reveal ways in which they marshal resources for making a decision when uncertain.

Ask them the following questions:

- What were your mechanisms for making that decision – avoidance, guess-work, reasoning, playfulness?
- How did your feelings change as the uncertainty lessened, and explanations were given?
- Were there elements of uncertainty that could be relished – because perhaps they provided scope for freedom?

Then ask them to consider whether they have similar reactions to more significant uncertainties. If so, they can identify a pattern and decide whether it is serving them well or whether they would like to make changes.

continued below

One of the features of the activity is that participants create their own context for dealing with the task. If the course is Creativity, they will tend to handle it creatively, or illuminate their own creative blocks. It puts trainees in touch with their own values and generally results in more appreciation for each other – particularly as they discover common interests, similar family patterns, the same hobbies, and shared feelings and values.

ACTIVITY ─────────────────────────────────

Finally, invite participants to make a wall or table gallery with the photos to form a reminder of their resources throughout the programme. If you wish, offer a simple action point or tip – for example, to keep the photos nearby afterwards, to provide an instant reminder of what's really important.

ENCOURAGING THE STRONG TO HELP THE WEAK (HARVESTING)

In traditional lecture courses, if someone knows the subject well, there is a danger they will become bored. If, instead, they are encouraged to teach the content to others, they can be engaged and helpful. From the trainer's point of view, a potential 'troublemaker' is transformed into a valued assistant. Their knowledge is validated, reinforced and they are quite clearly contributing.

When participants list their concerns, one of the most common worries is that they will have nothing to contribute. However, we can organize courses in such a way that everyone has something to offer.

One method is to have each trainee draw a mindmap, summarizing their knowledge of the subject. They then work in pairs to compare notes, explaining to the partner what extra bits they have included. An extension would be for each pair to split and form another pairing and share content again – continuing until everyone had reaped the collective harvest. This kind of pair-swapping also builds in an element of revision through repetition.

Another way for the stronger to help the weaker is for the trainer to organize coaching pairs within a course. Ideally, each partner will have a skill to transfer to the other, so no one feels generally weaker than another. The trainer should always stress the value of each participant. (The one who makes the most mistakes can be congratulated on providing the greatest number of learning opportunities.)

Of course, as the advanced student will want to gain something beyond their contribution – after all, they have not come primarily to tutor – it is good practice to find elements in the next session which will particularly challenge and stimulate these helpers.

On longer programmes, when colleagues continue to work together within their organization, encourage each participant to find a mentor. Mentoring is a system in which (usually) a more experienced practitioner partners and guides a less experienced colleague. (There are also companies in which mentoring takes a reverse pattern – junior colleagues provide counsel for senior personnel, as a listening ear or in some area of expertise.) A mentoring arrangement is a useful bridge between a training course and work at base.

Similarly, participants can form pairs – termed a 'buddy' system in the US – to work together between formal training events. Pairing is more likely to work well if people find their own partners rather than have them allocated. Give pairs the best chance of succeeding by introducing the idea several hours before putting it into action. This gives everyone the opportunity to assess the suitability of potential partners. Then set aside a few minutes later in the session to allow formal pair-making.

It is helpful to reduce the pressure of commitment by stating the minimum expectations of partnerships: 'The least you will have to do is to make contact by telephone one time before the course session next week. It's up to you if you want to take it further in the form of more calls, meetings or whatever. We'll be seeing how it goes, whether it is helpful, and will be reviewing next week, when you will have the opportunity to change partners without offence to whoever you are working with this week.'

In a pairs' session during a course, help each pair to structure their feedback for each other by asking them to confine themselves to telling each other what they have observed and what they have experienced. Direct them to avoid telling each other what they would have liked to have seen or what they believe the other should do. Advice is generally unwelcome unless requested.

When it works well, a pairs system provides considerable encouragement for implementing action points, allowing discussion and the surmounting of small difficulties between sessions. Any such stimulants to keep learning in the forefront boost your inspirational quotient.

MIXING THE NUMBERS

Each of us flourishes under different ways of working. We can help trainees discover which styles suit them by providing a range of opportunities. Some work best on their own, others in pairs or small groups, or in larger communities. Some like a variety of combinations.

Whatever the preferred learning style, the subject will often dictate the best form of teaching. A report-writing course will, at some point, involve the individual writer working alone. The Alexander Technique, which has an essential hands-on element, is best taught one-to-one with a teacher.

By contrast, language learning benefits from group work. This allows a variety of input, time for listening and reflection when others are on the spot, as well as the intensity of one-to-one instruction. Teambuilding also clearly requires working with the whole group together.

THE WORST AND BEST GAME

This process probes the group's resources and works well across many programmes. It contains:

- recollection;
- case studies;
- a chance to put bad experience behind us;
- extraction of learning from real experience;
- personal lessons in excellence.

Worst and Best

Ask the participants to recall their worst experience of being on the receiving end of the course subject. For instance, their worst experience of being managed, of being led, of being part of a team or of negotiating.

The exercise often starts with someone joking, 'There's plenty to choose from'. Within a few seconds, most trainees will have an example in mind. If anyone is having difficulty, suggest they choose between worst experiences from work, from a club or organization they belong to, or from their youth. They should choose either one outstanding incident or a period of time.

To forestall personal conflict, ask people to avoid using an example which reflects badly on anyone else in the room. It tends to raise issues beyond pure learning if your exemplar of worst management happens to be sitting next to you while you describe their shortcomings. Ask each participant to briefly describe their incident of worst practice. If there is time, they describe it to the whole group. With tighter deadlines, split them into smaller groups or pairs.

The facilitator (or listeners in the other version) takes notes, abstracting the elements that made this the worst practice and listing the consequences. If you are not certain what to write on the chart, ask the storyteller, 'What was it about it that made it the worst you have experienced?'

Worst practice of leadership – a typical flip-chart

Practices	*Consequences*
given deliberately false information	scheme went wrong, lost my job
dictatorial boss, no consultation	no commitment
manager took the credit	resentment

If you find the atmosphere darkening as the emotions associated with these incidents return from memory into the room, mention how poor practice in the past still has the power to make us feel bad even now. Add that fortunately we can distil the lessons from the past into a chart of 'what not to do'. And we know precisely the kind of impact it will have on our colleagues if we do in our turn what was done to us.

You might also mention that one of the classic ways in which poor practice is sustained is that unless we consciously decide otherwise, we tend to copy what was done to us. As parents, for example, our instinct is to do what our parents did. If they smacked, we smack. The second route is to rebel and do the opposite. This 'reactive parenting', in its way, has us just as much in thrall as direct copying. Only the third way – in which we are conscious of how we were treated, know that we are free to reconsider, and take the opportunity to do so – breaks the cycle.

State that in this exercise, as well as distilling learning from unpleasant memories, we have an opportunity to free ourselves from them. Simply expressing them can help in this process. You might even make a symbolic dustbin – tearing up the notes and stamping them into the ground – or use physical activity to discharge and transform the old negative energy. Shake it off, as the saying goes. This often proves pleasantly cathartic, and sets the stage for the second part of the process.

continued below

Simply the best

If there is time, it is preferable for the second part to be conducted with the whole group, rather than in pairs. By privileging 'best experience' – in that everyone hears everyone else's story in full – we reinforce the idea that this is what we are seeking.

ACTIVITY

Ask the group to consider the best experiences they have enjoyed as recipients of the subject under consideration, again delving into their memories to recall the time or occasion when they were best managed, led, translated, negotiated with and so on. As before, examples may be drawn from any aspect of work-life, home-life, clubs, school or college days. The important elements are the practices employed and the results experienced.

In groups of British managers, someone usually remarks that it was easy to think of poor instances, but more of a challenge to recall when they have been well-managed. Ask each participant to describe their best experience to the group and contribute a summarizing key word or phrase to the flipchart. If you demonstrated the key-wording on the 'worst practice' section, it is an elegant touch to hand over the scribing to each person presenting the 'best practice' notes. It adds a timely opportunity for people to present up-front, as they are usually feeling good at this point, basking in the glow of an empowering memory, and will tend to speak well. Building the trainees' confidence by giving them the opportunity to demonstrate unconscious skills such as performing spontaneously in front of a group is always worthwhile.

The generated list tends to include some words which may be interpreted either as qualities or practices. For example, 'trusting', 'sharing', 'clear communication', 'high expectation'.

We earn the right to be described as having a certain quality by regularly engaging in the relevant practice. If we keep trusting people, eventually we shall be called trusting. As managers, trainers or leaders, we are judged by what we do, by practice more than profession.

The activity produces solid, anecdotal evidence of what actually works.

Jan Carlzon provides a 'Best' incident of delegation and spontaneity, following a general election. 'No instruction manual could have detailed how to address a plane full of businessmen on the morning after a socialist victory. Allowed to take responsibility for the situation, however, the captain seized on a "moment of truth" that the passengers aren't likely to forget.' (Carlzon, 1987: 63.)

TRANSFERRING BEST PRACTICES INTO TRAINING PROGRAMME DESIGN

The Worst and Best activity consistently generates lists that look remarkably similar. Whatever the make-up of the group, people's motivators or demotivators tend to be the same.

Of course, it is possible that participants are in some way fooling themselves and that what actually works is different from what they believe and say works. But this is unlikely. The list is created by people recalling real occasions when they felt well (or badly) managed or led. They recall what was said and done in certain circumstances and how they reacted. If, in the first part, their reactions were actually to work better, they soon realize this and tend not to offer it as an example of poor management. Sophisticated ploys of contrary managers are analysed and discounted.

The 'best management' list usually shapes up along these lines:

- Good managers provide an inspiring vision and/or clear goals. Clarity is often stressed as particularly important: 'I knew exactly what was required'.
- The person managed subscribes to the vision.
- The person managed agrees to the goals. This is often through involvement in setting them: 'We'd agreed what I was to do.'
- The person is left to get on with the job. This is often in circumstances which struck them as particularly challenging.
- The manager expressed confidence that the person could deal with the job in hand and achieve pre-set goals.
- The manager was available for back-up when needed.
- The manager had an open-door policy. This was most graphically expressed in one organization where all managers had a private office protected by a traffic-light system. On red, no one could enter; amber indicated you would be allowed in soon; green meant you were free to walk in. The manager concerned kept his light constantly on green.
- There was an agreed checking procedure. Checks while the work was in progress were either at agreed stages or at the request of the worker.

Among the most commonly cited worst management practices are unnecessary interference and over-zealous monitoring – namely, ways in which the manager conveyed the belief that the worker was going to fail and therefore was not going to be trusted.

It is still surprisingly rare for managers to offer useful feedback to staff or even to explain how decisions were made. This matters because people who work in unresponsive, inflexible organizations are more dissatisfied with their jobs and suffer higher levels of stress than those who work in environments which promote effective, open communication at all levels.

All the 'best' elements led to feelings of empowerment and resulted in the person working more effectively than before. In particular, fond memories are often recalled of managers who were respected for their individual, personal qualities. These managers may have been managing in a style approved or determined by the organization, but they were certainly not perceived that way. An organization may be viewed with varying degrees of affection or contempt, but relationships with individual managers are what stand out.

So we are looking at human qualities, which – as the following list illustrates – can all be incorporated into your inspirational training.

Features to incorporate into inspirational training

Feature	Trainer Includes
Vision	Big picture of post-programme scenario, things working well.
Clear goals	New skills/knowledge directed towards deployment on the job
Subscription/involvement	An opportunity for trainees to share in goal-setting for the course itself and afterwards.
Be allowed to get on with the task in hand	Processes with minimal supervision.
Back-up	Personal accessibility.

INVISIBILITY

As you develop your repertoire, confidence and wisdom, take more risks, such as extending greater trust to participants.

On one Leadership course, a delegate complained that the trainers were apparently doing nothing. She stated that they should be doing more to earn their fees. Having checked that she was improving her performance as a leader, the trainers decided to take her comments as a compliment.

If you risk losing a client because of your 'invisibility', it may be worth explaining what you are doing and what you are not doing, and that you plan to allow the participants to practise empowering themselves. This principle is most apparent at the heart of Train the Trainer programmes, where handing-over is a critical element.

OPEN SESSIONS

You build confidence when you demonstrate your trust. This can be achieved in small ways such as allowing participant input into rules, assuming they will return from breaks in good time and complete processes without excess supervision.

You can go further by turning part of the course design and delivery over to them in the form of open sessions. A typical open session might last a half-day or a full day, perhaps within a multi-day programme.

Tell participants that part of the timetable will be handed over to them, so that they can offer sessions to each other. You could indicate that these are to be exchanges of skills or discussions on particular topics.

Participants' skill share

Part of the format of the management development course for a broadcasting organization was to allow the twelve trainees to divide one day between them. Anyone wishing to offer a session put up a notice, with a brief description and proposed running time.

Participants signed their name to any session that appealed, and those with no sign-ups were abandoned. The day was then timetabled between the others, with choices at certain points. People were now free to attend any session, without regard to the earlier sign-ups, and if someone wanted a break or to work on their own, that was also permitted.

One typical set of choices included:

- instruction in directing a three-camera set-up for a live news broadcast;
- stress management;
- samba dancing (taught by a Brazilian broadcaster on secondment);
- creativity techniques.

Each session reflected more or less strongly the main themes of the management course – the samba dancing as a means of team-building, for example. Yet each was presented from a completely different base of knowledge, experience and perspective than the regular course trainers could have offered. The styles ranged from simple lecture, to workshop session, to a full simulation in a news studio.

Open sessions draw on the expertise of each leader and imbue the group with confidence in their own abilities – as holders of valid experience which can be passed to others.

Recipients of the skills tend to be keen to support the leaders. Everyone knows that they may lack experience as trainers, but have volunteered themselves to offer something to their colleagues, despite minimal time for preparation. This, too, builds group cohesion and generates confidence in session leaders.

It naturally also takes confidence on the part of the official trainers to hand over to participants in this way. The evidence suggests it is a risk worth taking.

Taking this principle to its limit, whole programmes are sometimes designed as open sessions or completely self-managed events. Here the trainers become facilitators setting up a framework, and acting as resources and referees. After an ice-breaker and a discussion on rules and agreements, the facilitator hands over to the delegates, who decide what to talk about, how to organize themselves and what methods of reporting back they prefer.

These sessions go under various names, including Open Space (developed by Harrison Owen), Café Society and skillshares. The particular rules of each variant are less important than the attitude of the facilitator towards the concept. If you believe the self-managed open session will work, you will convey that belief to participants and make success more likely.

THE RESOURCE GALLERY

Delegates often enjoy recalling their accomplishments in the resource gallery. Deploy this for projects when personal resources are an issue – perhaps when staff recognize that they are facing a stiff challenge and also when they need to pool resources for the benefit of a team. It offers discovery and mutual appreciation of what everyone is bringing to the party.

ACTIVITY

Pride park

Provide plenty of large sheets of paper and a variety of felt tips, crayons, pencils and pens.

Create a relaxed atmosphere in which each participant recalls an achievement of which they are particularly proud – one of the finest things they have ever done, perhaps the best – something that called upon and really stretched their inner resources.

Their task is to draw that achievement – and here you should stress that there are no marks for graphic skills. Any level of pictorial ability will do, and stick figures are fine. The important point is to capture the achievement in an image. This may take about ten minutes.

Towards the end of the time, suggest that the 'artists' write on the same page a list of the qualities and personal resources they needed for this achievement. They can avoid undue modesty by taking the perspective of an impressed outsider.

When the artwork is finished, the pictures are stuck on the walls, and everyone tours the gallery, with each in turn saying anything they wish about their achievement.

The tales are generally inspiring, and whether they involve passing driving tests, climbing mountains, exotic travel, managing a divorce or staying in touch with children, each is meaningful to the protagonist and usually of interest to colleagues. If teamwork is an issue, a variant is to allow work-mates to add qualities they have perceived to each other's lists.

Participants are now likely to be in the mood to do the creative work of deciding how they plan to apply these resources to current challenges.

PAYBACK AT WORK

By drawing deeply on the group's resources, we are likely to make their learning time more closely resemble pertinent aspects of organizational reality. Back at base, participants may not have the luxury of sitting comfortably and absorbing valuable lessons. They will be dealing with complex combinations of people and circumstances, requiring applications of all their resources. Good organizations seek to stretch their personnel with demanding yet manageable challenges.

By assuming that trainees have the necessary resources, and discovering their current levels of ability and achievement, we can pitch our training to match need with capability.

INSPIRATIONS

- Find out what the participants already know and, whenever possible, start from there.
- Harvest the know-how in the room, by encouraging the strong to help the weak.
- Consider mentoring, coaching or buddy pairs to reinforce learning both during and between sessions.
- Participants typically can draw many of the lessons of a programme from their own previous experience.
- Take more risks by handing over as much of the programme to participants as you dare.

10

Spontaneity

A principal aim of inspirational training is to encourage spontaneity in ourselves and our trainees. Paradoxically, spontaneity can be taught, and offers us the means for dealing with all kinds of eventualities.

Inspirational training is powered by the volatile fuel of spontaneity. As we stay with the awareness of the moment, we ride the waves of energy as the moment itself changes, and we remain spontaneous, reacting and interacting with whatever we encounter. Like a surfer, it is all too easy to be distracted and to fall. But once we have experienced the rush of spontaneity, we will tend to seek it out again and, knowing how to recognize it, begin to master it. Such mastery may be:

- instinctive and natural, which is the way children live spontaneously until taught otherwise;
- rediscovered, by eliminating the blocks to spontaneity;
- learnt through principles, which we can consciously apply, using a variety of techniques.

PRINCIPLES AND TECHNIQUES

It may seem paradoxical to speak of techniques for spontaneity but, through the application of the techniques, one can reach a point at which pure spontaneity takes over.

Why do we need spontaneity? For ourselves as trainers and learners, it enables us to handle whatever comes up, riding over the bumps which are inevitable in any but the most predictable training situations. As philosopher James P Carse puts it (1987): 'To be prepared against surprise is to be trained. To be prepared for surprise is to be educated'.

Spontaneity sharpens our receptivity, so we can learn new skills and be open to new experience, and it widens our range, so that we grow. Improvisation is a way of opening the intake door – an alternative to blocking the many signals which are available to us. We find improvisation in many traditions, from jazz music, clowning and storytelling to Indian 'ragas' – lengthy pieces which begin with musicians tuning their instruments to the vibrations of the room they are in and their audience. One essential element is the delight which comes from making things up; another is the importance of doing it on the spot – here and now, with each performance fresh for, and responsive to, the situation.

Creators in each of these fields devise games and structures to contain – and so allow the expression of – spontaneity. The extra risk and uncertainty of staying in a continuous present makes every moment dynamic and more exciting.

Trainees benefit from our spontaneity. They enjoy truly witty dialogue and fresh exchanges. Prepared lines are good, but those which could not have been scripted are often better. They make a course palpably unique, and win the devotion of participants as they appreciate that your responses are particular to them.

I once saw a trainer role-playing a drunk, abusive questioner to help teach a presenter to deal with difficult audiences. His outburst was met with the presenter responding, 'You are disturbing my talk. Please leave and report to the managing director'. To which the trainer replied, 'I am the managing director'.

Without spontaneity, things become dull. Audiences quickly sense when they are watching a play that has suffered too many performances, a speech with too many repetitions, a training course that is exactly the same time after time.

Accept and build

Inspirational training turns constructively adventurous when players apply the principles of 'accepting' and 'building'.

Accepting consists of saying 'yes' – whether explicitly or implicitly. It means going along with what it first suggested. You may have experienced something of this nature in a brainstorming session when, for the benefit of the process, you temporarily suspended criticism.

Many people find it hard to accept. They have been trained from very early days to oppose. Because they believe that they have always gained more ground by argument, they fail to appreciate the possibilities of agreement and co-operation. Others are comfortable with saying 'yes', as long as they can follow it immediately with 'but'. At its best, the idea of 'but' is to keep the good parts of the premise, then slice away the weaknesses. At its worst, 'but' is a thinly-veiled mechanism for disagreement or not listening.

In 'building', we accept the 'yes' completely, and add 'and'. Each successive 'and' strengthens the edifice. There is no destruction, slicing or going back.

This is the way actors extemporize instant scenes, by pushing the ramification of an idea towards its limits, whether dramatic or comic. The surrealistic British comedian Eddie Izzard uses improvisational thought in his solo shows. He muses that the sound of cats purring actually means they are drilling. It is an amusing idea, which he extends for a while – they are drilling for gold, oil, anything really, it's just in their nature. Then he builds: the drilling is secret, and if we ask our cats they will deny it – 'Drilling? No, I'm a cat' – and later he goes a step further towards an apparently illogical absurdity by describing how he caught out his cat by finding its drilling equipment.

Of course, it is possible to refine the fruits of such improvisation – by editing. We brainstorm, then assess the ideas, but it is important to note that the editing is a separate process, and is best kept for a separate session (or part of a session). When colleagues refrain from premature evaluation, it engenders valuable experiences of trust and commitment. We move swiftly together into the unknown.

When not following the principles of 'accept' and 'build', people tend instead to block. Blocking is most easily spotted by use of negative words like 'not' and 'never', and by negative constructions, 'No; I can't; won't.'

Blocking may be a direct refusal to go along with the first suggestion. Subtler blocking is to say 'Yes, but'. 'But' is an overused conjunction in modern newspapers, often repositories of cynicism. And creative blocking (but blocking nonetheless) is to counter-propose. 'Let's go to Swindon' met with 'Let's go to Millwall'.

When someone blocks, the improvisational craft gets stuck. The negative idea damages the impetus, and the proponents of spontaneity may feel vulnerable and discouraged.

Blocking
    Let's open a new factory.
    No, it's too expensive.
    (Result – argument, or things stay the same.)

Accept and Build
> Let's open a new factory.
> Yes, and we'll have the latest machines.
> *(Result – opening up the conversation to many possibilities.)*

Blocking with 'Yes, but'
> I see you have a new photocopier.
> Yes, but you can't use it.
> *(Result – frustration or argument.)*

Accept and Build
> I see you have a new photocopier.
> Yes, and if you press this button. . .
> *(Result – a different style of answer, leading to new ideas and actions.)*

Here and now

When we work with 'accepting' and 'building', we rapidly extend the territory of an idea. It is also possible to develop the details of the new, shared concept by attending to the 'here and now'. This involves focus and scoping.

Suppose you want to design a more efficient office environment with your staff. You can use a 'here and now' activity to help the design process. The office and its immediate surroundings are the 'here', and the activity is to explore mentally and physically as many aspects of this area as you can. Occupy the space, walk around, examine it, touch the walls, find the nooks and crannies, and allow whatever you observe to prompt the imagination to new possibilities. The participants can work individually or discuss ideas in groups.

While they do so, it is important for them to avoid defining the 'here' too narrowly. This means it is acceptable and even desirable to allow similes, comparisons and brief forays to neighbouring areas.

They may find it helpful to keep in mind the broader idea of 'this world' – the domain that is the subject of the exercise. The 'here' is purely physical territory, whereas 'this world' is the conceptual framework you choose to cover that territory. In our office example, the office space is the 'here', and the combination of the organization, the people and the office is 'this world'. In other words, during the activity the participants are aware of the context of the space, and they might turn their ideas towards new applications of existing equipment, alternatives to desks, re-allocation of flooring, enhancing the air-space and a wondrous range of recycling.

You can also apply 'here' to prevent unhelpful wandering of the imagination during training activities. If there is an important discussion between colleagues, for example, an insistence on 'here' will centre it on those present and on their communications with each other.

The companion to 'here' is 'now', which adds immediate time to immediate space. Remind trainees to 'stay in the moment', to draw the most benefit from whatever is going on right now.

How can you 'stay in the moment'? Try these:

- Focus through listening.
- Remain aware of the present.
- Don't anticipate.
- Don't plan ahead – for example, by trying to steer.

The inability to stay present in time robs us of vitality. To change for the future we need to catch up to the present.

Some processes benefit from a rhythm. Yet often the effect of a rhythm is trance-like and takes people away from awareness of the present. Break rhythms. Insist on irregular timing whenever you want to bring people back to a consciousness of what they are doing.

As participants find during the One Word sequence below, sometimes conscious thinking is too slow. Ruth Zaporah (1995) writes: 'Whatever we think up lacks freshness. When we're thinking – as opposed to listening to ourselves with less attachment and staying with each moment – we never get beyond ourselves and the familiar.'

Freedom within structure

'Here and now' creates structure, a framework within which there is freedom to take many routes – including those which alter the structure itself. Structure is like grammar. Each sentence that conforms to the grammar of a language fits the structure, yet within a simple structure we find infinite possibilities. In many art forms, the more refined and seemingly constricting the structure, the greater the freedom experienced by the artist. It is as if too much 'freedom' in unstructured forms results in feelings of not knowing what to do next. A novel, for example, has looser requirements than strict verse. And free verse has (arguably) hardly any structural requirements by comparison with either.

We find similar patterns in sport. In 1996 footballer Jimmy Case said this about the Liverpool championship-winning team in which he played:

Once you were on the pitch you had a certain role to play but they always gave you some freedom. They realized that, to be a footballer, you've got to have something about you – like an instinct – where, if something unexpected presents itself, then you'll have the ability and the skill to deal with it. . .

It is possible to think of training as a way of refining structures in order to create and allow the examination of pertinent freedoms. If you are training pilots, for example, and the chosen aspect is the handling of controls, it makes sense to use a simulator so that the pilot gets the chance to practise responding to all sorts of stimuli. You do not need to put passengers at risk for this exercise, so by using a simulator you remove the currently irrelevant element. If you want to improve sales techniques, you use role-plays or the rehearsals for success described in the next chapter, so removing the genuine customers who you cannot afford to lose if unimpressed with untrained salespeople.

One-word sequences

The One-word sequence gives participants a feel for 'accept and build' and 'here and now' and, for most, is an enjoyable dip into spontaneity. Typical experiences within the process lead logically to considerations of improved communication, particularly when key issues are teamwork or leadership.

While you can play with as few as two participants, it is excellent with about eight, then gradually loses impact with increasing numbers as people have to wait too long for their next active involvement. So I advise splitting 12 delegates or more into groups.

The main aims of the first part of the process are to:

- raise alertness;
- bond the group through achieving a task together;
- introduce principles of communication, particularly to repair 'damage' when communication breaks down.

ACTIVITY

Communication activity – One-word circle
Begin with the group in a circle. It generally works better standing than sitting, producing a higher-energy level, particularly for first-timers.

Introduce a soft ball, which is thrown gently under-arm from person to person in any order. If you don't have a ball, or when you feel the

---

group is ready to work faster, create an equivalent sequence by pointing: anyone pointed at points to someone else in the circle.

The structure by now should be apparent, and relatively simple. If the ball is being dropped or fought over, or if the pointing sequence is breaking down, then stop the game to sort out the communication problem.

continued below

While learning occurs throughout the activity, the breakdowns are the best times for stating learning points. For example, in the throwing sequence, it might be necessary to make a rule explicit: namely not to throw until the person is ready to receive.

It may be useful to bring assumptions to the surface – stating, for example, that the sender needs to know how to judge that the receiver is ready. Generally the receiver will indicate readiness, by nodding or accepting eye contact.

Sometimes the pointing variation breaks down when two people simultaneously react as if the point were to them. How can the group solve the overspill? Either by more exact pointing (greater effort on the part of the communicator), or more elegantly by improving the structure – by making the circle more circular.

ACTIVITY

When the circle is operating smoothly, introduce the idea that each person will speak one word, chosen spontaneously. The structure makes it helpfully hard to plan, because you can't predict your turn – it comes only at the moment when someone throws (or points) to you.

The word is said while the ball is in the air on its way to the participant. The arc of the ball ('spontaneity space') defines the short time available to select and utter their word.

If they catch the ball before they speak, they have taken too long. If this happens a couple of times, then take a few moments in a smaller group – perhaps one-to-one with you – to practise. Almost everyone can manage this within a few attempts.

It is a good idea to switch from throwing to pointing after a while, because the participants may be distracted when they drop the ball. The ball's key function is to introduce the idea of speedy response. The rule now is 'When you are pointed at, say a word and point at someone else'.

> The first couple of rounds can be random words. Then suggest word association. Next introduce grammar – so that each word connects to the previous word to form a sentence.
>
> *continued on page 160*

When the activity is running smoothly, the group creates sentence after sentence to form stories. Any story is possible. When it goes well, the group will delight itself with its surprising wit and coherence, creating a real sense of bonding and collective successful enterprise. You might helpfully model useful words for starting sentences in this game, which include 'The', 'My', 'Once', 'Whenever' and 'Three'.

All the stories are disposable. Any time a story breaks down, the participants mentally throw it away and launch into the next. Whether or not you go straight into the next story depends on the reason for the breakdown, and what learning points you wish to extract from the exercise. Here are some of the possibilities:

- Someone can't think of a word and is silent. Suggest there is always a word in their mind and that they can say the first word they think of. There are no rights or wrongs. Next time round they are unlikely to suffer the same reaction.
- Someone can't think of a word and starts explaining this with more than one word. Suggest as above, pointing out that they had several words to choose from. Request that they turn their attention for the moment from 'discussing' to 'doing'.
- The sentence is so complex that it no longer makes grammatical sense. Allow it to end anywhere, or stop it yourself, saying, 'I've lost it'.
- The current word isn't heard. Ask the group to solve it. They usually want the quiet person to speak louder, or they find a way to reduce the volume of distractions.
- Everyone is laughing to a point of collapse. Pause.

When the group has succeeded in telling some stories, however rudimentary, end the game or move it on to the Three-Person Expert activity before the energy flags.

Three-Person Expert

Three-Person Expert serves as an exercise in presentation, team building or product improvement. A skilled inspirational trainer will also adapt it to meet other objectives by emphasizing the particular facets which are most relevant to the learning points required.

Three-Person Expert adds a performance element when you split the group into audience and players. Arrange the performing area so that an 'interviewer' faces a row of three chairs, or a bench on which three interviewees sit closely together.

Three-Person Expert

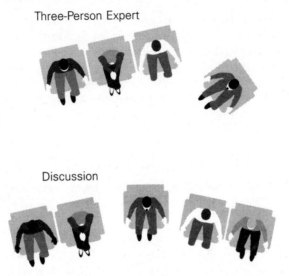

Discussion

Figure 10.1 *Layouts for Three-Person Expert*

ACTIVITY

Explain that the interviewees are to speak one word each at a time, as in the previous exercise, only now they take turns beginning with the closest to the interviewer, then the one in the middle, then the one on the end, and back round again in this same circular sequence. They are to consider themselves as 'of one mind', and imagine themselves to be expert on whatever subject comes up.

The interviewer finds a topic at random (perhaps by soliciting a suggestion from the audience), and asks the 'guest' a question. Typically a first question might be 'When did you start gardening?' or 'Could you please begin by defining astrology?' When the panel finishes answering a question, one word at a time, the interviewer asks another.

The product is the performance. A good product holds and amuses the audience. A poor product bores or frustrates them. The teamwork between the three panellists and between the panel and questioner determines the quality.

After a few exchanges, stop the interview and ask the performers and audience how the product could be improved. Depending on time, either allow the same team to implement the suggestions or swap players around. I always opt for swaps, as the main benefits arise from everyone having a turn on the one-word panel. It is here that they experience the power of spontaneity within a team, and begin to appreciate 'flow', as without pauses for thought the words speed up and the answers captivate your audience.

After each break, change the topic to maintain spontaneity by preventing preplanning.

Groups generally offer many suggestions for enhancing the performance, and most are easy enough for the players to put into practice. The ones that tend to work best are variants of 'here and now' for the panel and 'accept and build' for the questioner.

Depending on time and the size of your group, it is possible to allow more people to have a go by having two teams of either two or three, mediated by the questioner in a discussion. In this version, the skilful questioner avoids leading the teams into direct debate, instead guiding both into contributing to a discussion, perhaps by having one 'amateur' and one 'professional' with respect to the topic.

Disposability

Disposability is an important facet of improvisation. We are seeking structures which make it easy (and painless) to sift what matters (and may be kept) from what doesn't (and is therefore disposable).

In the Three-Person Expert stories, for example, what matter are factors like speed and continuity, rather than information of dubious quality about chicken farming. The stories themselves are disposable, which is one reason for choosing any subject, rather than selecting, say, topics from the course.

For inspirational trainers there are no mistakes. Participants simply do what they do, which may or may not yield tangible results. One's beliefs become temporarily irrelevant. This is disconcerting for some and liberating for others. Personal agendas can easily distract us from awareness of the present. We start judging the moment against the agenda and, in so doing, the moment is lost or at least diluted. Instead of experiencing the constant flow of change – which we may reflect on later – we allow beliefs to govern our actions, reducing our chances of learning anything.

The wise trainer constructs an arena where there's no such thing as a false move. If participants insist on judging certain actions as mistakes, then they can enjoy the training programme as the perfect place to make them. Gradually they may appreciate that perfectionism is a block to learning and to creativity. And that each moment holds everything they need to meet the next moment.

Perfectionism

There is a saying that 80 per cent is perfection. As trainers, this is a useful guide. If we operated at 100 per cent (as if we could!), we would probably intimidate participants and risk feeling too pleased with ourselves – apart from making no mistakes to learn from, leaving nothing to strive for.

If we dispose of the need to get everything 'right', we will be more spontaneous and more creative. Hamlet, with the help of William Shakespeare, says, 'There is nothing either good or bad, but thinking makes it so'. One of the troubles with perfectionism is it can stop you from getting started. You restrict your range of activities to those where you feel sufficient chance of 'success'. You might refuse to try a new game, sport or hobby – or more critically, to fulfil your deeper ambitions – in case you are no good at them. Well, the chances are that you won't be much good to start with. There is no shame in being a beginner.

Another block to creativity is channelling all activity directly towards the 'right' result. Comedian Arnold Brown describes Scottish biologist Alexander Fleming's discovery of penicillin on a culture which he had left overnight: 'If he'd been English, he'd just have cleared up the mess'.

The nine aids described below reveal some ways of jettisoning perfectionism and will lend a more experimental, improvisational quality to your work.

┌─ **I**NSPIRATIONS ─────────────────

Nine aids to overcoming perfectionism

1. 'Whose standards are they anyway?' Your idea of satisfactory may be as valid as that of the person demanding perfection. Or if you are the perfectionist, you could work to someone else's less demanding standard. They may only want one instant suggestion, not three well worked feasibility studies.
2. 'Good enough' can be better than perfect. Others are less likely to be resentful and jealous. A training course is an opportunity to practise imperfection in small ways and enjoy your new freedom.

3. The first 20 per cent of effort often achieves 80 per cent of the solution. As diminishing returns set in, the most efficient thing to do is to stop early. Aim for satisfaction rather than perfection.
4. A 'failure' can often be considered a 'success' in that it reveals a way not to do something or a step towards doing something else.
5. You can't always know the results of your actions. The unpredictable outcomes of less-than-perfect may be the best part of a project. Art often resides in the flaws.
6. Perfection as a goal creates pressure and stress. Any lapse destroys the chance of achieving it. Aiming for excellence is healthier than aiming for perfection and excellence has the bonus of being achievable more often.
7. There is no 7. This list is imperfect.
8. Less-than-perfect leaves room for improvement.
9. When perfection means doing it all yourself, you miss all the benefits of delegation, collaboration and team-work.

Effort or indirection

One of the most successful inspirational training strategies is to trust in successful outcomes. Paradoxically, effort can be counterproductive, but there are ways to make things easier.

When being spontaneous:

- your first thought is the one to go with (for the moment);
- appreciate the 'power of the obvious';
- remember to deal with the process and allow content to look after itself.

In instinctive mode, the first thought is almost always at least as good as the second, third or fourth, and by definition it is quicker. It is also likely to be the most obvious, and the obvious is often exactly what is required. The great temptation is to try to be clever (less obvious), which takes time, talent and frequently fails.

In the One-word sequence, less effort brings more reward. Trying hard with furrowed brow and concentration doesn't work because there is too much going on for anyone to succeed in handling it consciously.

Many tasks are best dealt with on the edges of consciousness, where they become semi-automatic. Follow the movement and attend to the question, without fearing the outcome or aiming directly for the goal.

The principle of indirection is useful for trainers, who can set tasks whereby concentration on one thing leads to achievement of another. Flow is often found through creative distraction.

In teambuilding, for example, you might use the Telepathy activity below, where conscious attention can be directed towards listening, in order to reach the 'goal' of the countdown. (The underlying goal may be team-building or to improve communication skills, but the immediate aim is a smooth count.)

ACTIVITY

Telepathy

Players sit back to back. The aim is to count from 1 to 20, one number at a time. Anyone can speak at any time. But if two people speak simultaneously – however fleetingly – they start again from one.

There is no set order of turns. The players have to judge the moment to safely speak when no one else will speak. As the group attunes, so they improve at reaching 20 with fewer restarts.

Variants are to sit facing each other, or at greater distances, or in any mixture of positions. Eyes can be shut to make it trickier. When 20 is reached, a fresh challenge is to count down again to one.

The count is generally achieved more easily than you might imagine. It provides a great sense of achievement to the group – precisely because it seems so unlikely. Sometimes the game is frustrating and takes many attempts, so make sure there is enough flexibility in the timetable to allow completion. It is rare for a group to give up before succeeding in this challenge.

RESPONSIBILITY

Many inspirational training activities raise the issue of responsibility. Who is responsible for the outcome of the game? Who is the leader? The answer is usually that everyone has some responsibility and that leadership switches from person to person. Clearly, this is a useful message for much modern organizational working.

I once played Telepathy with a group which had a very forceful leader who counted the whole sequence himself. His tone of voice and raised finger indicated that no one was to interrupt. It was a strategy which worked –

and probably could continue to work – in the short term. The downside, we could point out, not only includes the waste of talent because no one else is contributing, but also the fact that no one else will be used to taking responsibility, when for example the leader tires (or in real life, leaves or retires).

If a leader is reluctant to share responsibility, sometimes participants need to take it. One of the roles of a manager is to make decisions. In drama improvisations, there is a rule of thumb which is 'no wimping'. It means that if you are participating in an exercise, engage in it fully. In a storytelling game, for example, you might face a junction point at which a verb is the next obvious word. A wimping choice is to say 'decided to' and leave the more significant content to the next person. The stronger player makes a commitment and says 'leaped', 'attacked', 'escaped' or whatever. Wimps say 'very' instead of taking responsibility for an adjective.

In a team where all take responsibility, stories (and by extension, other products) consist only of their essentials and tend to be more satisfying for listeners (or consumers).

The burden of responsibility is lighter when it is shared. These improvisational activities have participants practise sharing responsibility and trust-building, which flourishes when players feel that others are pulling their weight.

CREATIVITY

People who absorb the lessons of 'here and now' and 'accept and build', and are willing to improvise, tend to be more creative. Their creativity flourishes as they do less (in training or real-life performance), relax and let go of the future. Good actors, for example, create presence by simplifying, and they achieve this through focused attention. More attention to the moment enhances their creativity.

There is a choice of starting-points here: relaxed awareness leading to activity, or activity prompting relaxed awareness. Alternatively, we can use both, switching between Target and Try It.

Target is about visions and values and knowing what you want to create. This works for some creators and is part of the models propounded by Stephen Covey (1992): 'start with the end in mind'; and Robert Fritz (1989).

While this kind of goal-based approach is clearly effective with many people, others do better with Try It, acting on their first impulses and then discovering or deciding where the activity is leading. Many writers, actors and painters work in this way. The inspiration is somehow released only when they begin to work with their materials.

If you start with Try It, there's less risk of feeling that your efforts have gone wrong. Worry is suspended during the Try It phase. Things apparently simply happen.

We can assess Try It by switching to Target. If our creation falls short of the target, we can nevertheless sense progress and try again. Both approaches work well. What is helpful is to understand how we – or our trainees – operate and where they are in the cycles of creative progress.

EXPECTING THE UNEXPECTED

'It's the uncertainty of sport that keeps us watching', said British TV presenter Des Lynam. The possibility of an upset or anticipation of a closely-fought contest maintains our attention. It is the sense of imminent disaster that rivets our attention to the tightrope walker.

Improvisational techniques allow us to play with uncertainty without being overwhelmed by it. Because it is linked with wit, you can tell when improvisation is taking place by the laughter in the atmosphere. This is good for the participants' health and for relationships, and has beneficial impacts on learning.

Spontaneity will bring your sessions to life. As this is the greatest advantage available to the live trainer, you should maximize this asset. It is where we add the most value.

█NSPIRATIONS

- Amongst the many routes to spontaneity are instinct, rediscovery and the application of principles.
- Spontaneity keeps things alive, exciting and fun.
- Say 'yes', and add 'and' to accept and build – this is the impro-visational route to creativity.
- There is always freedom within a structure, but we are not always aware of it or ready to exercise that freedom.
- Use the activities in this chapter to give participants experiences of improvising, creating and being in 'spontaneity space'.
- Avoid perfectionism, mix Target and Try It.

11

Rehearsals for success

Relish question sessions and turn role-plays and simulations into effective means of actively preparing delegates for complex, important challenges.

As you gain confidence, you develop the ability to respond to circumstances. Your sessions become more flexible and you can extend elements of inspirational training into more areas of your work.

A QUESTION OF FEAR

Some trainers are happy to deliver their lectures or run processes with which they are familiar, but fear questions from participants. Others are ready to allow questions at almost any time, which helps trainees feel relaxed and able to participate at will, without concern that they have misunderstood something and are not permitted to ask. The latter approach clearly aids learning.

Some common fears that inhibit presenters from welcoming questions include:

- fear of not knowing the answer;
- fear of knowing the answer but being unable to access it in the heat of the moment;
- fear that our lack of knowledge will be exposed;
- fear of our embarrassment if it is apparent that the trainees know more than we do;
- fear that the question will be a conduit for hostility or other emotions that we may prefer to avoid facing;
- fear of the expectation that we will be witty;
- fear of taking too much time and wrecking the schedule.

Perhaps trainers have something to learn from politicians who relish questions, realizing that they are an opportunity to put their case as if invited, which leaves a better impression than imposing on the audience.

A simple tool for dealing with questions is to respond with the following sequence – the CEA strategy:

Clarify – Emotion – Answer

Clarify

When someone asks a question, the trainer begins by restating it to clarify it in the minds of:

- the audience;
- the questioner;
- the trainer.

Each is important, and by simplifying, repeating or rephrasing we ensure that everyone in the room is dealing with the same point. It is important for the audience because they may not have heard what the questioner asked. It is less so for the questioner, although the sharpening of the question by the lecturer can be helpful if they have phrased it in a complex way or are unsure of what they want to know. And it is good for the trainer preparing to answer the question as it buys a little time, so that the brain can order thoughts and recall facts. This is also the easiest part of the response, which helps quell fears and calm any panics.

Clarifying can be as simple as repeating the questioner's exact words or it can reframe the question in such a way as to take the whole audience into our sweep: 'The gentleman is asking. . .', 'The question is. . .' or 'What Mrs Jones wants to know is. . .'.

Another option is a more radical restatement of the question. This is how politicians use questions to set themselves up to deliver only the information they want to provide.

Suppose a questioner launches into a tirade about dangers on the railways since new regulations came into force. The politician begins the response with 'This is a concern about safety on the railways' and is immediately on comfortable territory about measures taken, rather than dangers left not dealt with or arguments about the merits of the regulations themselves.

Vague or multipoint questions can be answered in many different ways. We can use clarification to point us – and the audience – in the direction we propose to take during our answer.

Emotion

The second phase of the response takes us outside the content of the question to deal with any emotions stirring within the questioner, the audience and the lecturer. Our concern here is with emotional pitch, with the force of delivery and with the assent the query gathers – or fails to gather – from the rest of the audience. It is an opportunity to empathize or confront.

During the emotion phase of our response we might say:

- 'That's a very good question.'
- 'I'm often asked that.'
- 'That's the first time I've been asked that.'
- 'I can tell this is a very important matter for you.'
- 'Many of us have worried about this aspect.'
- 'I find that a very tricky area.'
- 'This question reaches the heart of the matter.'
- 'What an outrageous question!'

What we are doing is neutralizing the questioner, by showing the appropriate emotional response before giving our answer. On a contentious topic, we could say, 'There are many views about this – you clearly have yours. I shall now tell you mine'.

This is a strategy for avoiding conflict. The clarify and answer sections of the response are directed primarily at the audience as a whole. The emotion part is aimed principally at the questioner.

Answer

Clarifying and dealing with emotion have cleared the way for the final part of the response – the answer. Give the necessary information, succinctly.

When we don't know the answer, we may be tempted to waffle. It is better to say, 'I don't know the answer to that question'. We might add that we are willing to find out, and will do so later, or to say that we know someone who can provide it and will give contact details as appropriate. But we do not have to have all the answers.

If you are happy for a general discussion to begin, you can ask whether anyone in the room is able to reply. Alternatively, you might, perhaps with permission, invite a specialist in the audience to assist you with that particular question. Be aware that it changes the nature of the occasion from lecture plus question-and-answer into a more diffuse format. You change roles from lecturer to facilitator in that instant.

Many speakers make the mistake of addressing all parts of their response exclusively to the questioner. This is understandable, as we know that here at least is one person who wants the answer. The problem is that the group is still in session. We need to broaden the issue to include the group, while still taking care of the questioner's needs.

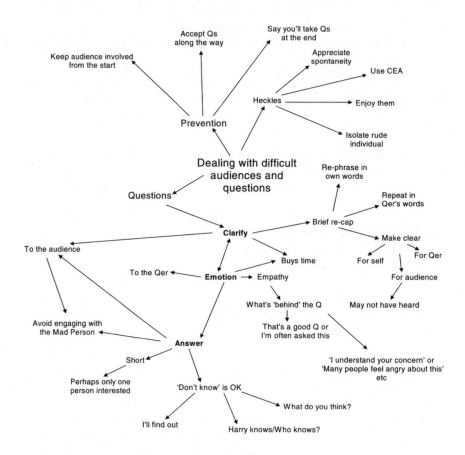

Figure 11.1 *Dealing with difficult questions and answers*

Broadening the response and making sure we include everyone has other benefits. We can monitor the general level of interest and, if we perceive a lack of interest in this particular question, but it requires a long answer, we can say, 'We must move on now, but I'll meet you afterwards to give you a fuller response'. It also helps to ensure that we don't 'tangle with the Mad Person'. The Mad Person is the aggressive or insinuating questioner who will give you trouble if given the opportunity. It is our job not to give that opportunity, and the CEA strategy minimizes it. We offer a chance to engage if we ask for the question to be repeated, if we check directly with that person whether we have understood that question, or if we address the whole response in their direction. Maintain the feeling that there's a whole group involved here, and that the benefit of the session is for all: any individual is asking on behalf of at least several members of the party.

Of course there is always the chance that the question interests only the person asking it (and perhaps the lecturer), so it is sound policy to keep answers short. Be deliberately brief. The question is not an invitation to restate chunks of the lecture.

It is your responsibility to shape the nature of question time. Decide whether or not it is indefinite; you can encourage your listeners by saying, 'I'm sure you have lots of questions', or keep them brief by stating, 'I have time for only two or three questions'. With questions, you set the agenda.

As you familiarize yourself with this structure in practice, so you will be able to do increasingly more within it. Once you have confidence in the CEA strategy, you can choose to follow the guidelines or depart from them as you feel appropriate.

THE TRAINER AS GYMNAST

Trainers are like gymnasts, learning to work pieces of equipment – the structures. First comes familiarization, perhaps a few gentle swings, then a more ambitious leap, next a skilled display in which all eyes are entirely on the amazing feats, relegating the equipment – or structure – completely to the background.

It is a pleasure to watch skilled performers at work. As audience members, we feel more confident when the artiste exhibits confidence. As performers, when we feel mastery over one arena, we are more than ready to enter the next.

If handling difficult questions is the vaulting horse, then more complex scenarios, such as simulations and rehearsals, are the floor exercises: they require more space and time, and provide more possibility and challenge.

The idea of rehearsal is familiar from theatre, and the idea of practice is readily accepted in sport. 'You cannot learn football by playing matches', said the Manchester United championship-winning manager Alex Ferguson. 'Playing matches doesn't make great footballers, practice does.'

Businesses, too, are increasingly appreciating the benefits of rehearsal and practice. Leaders are realizing that people do not learn simply by doing. For learning to occur, 'doing' is only one part of a process which also includes instruction, reflection and opportunities to experiment.

While it is possible to achieve much by reflection, review and deciding to change one's actions, it is possible to achieve more by also practising the changes before employing them in the 'real world'.

THE PURPOSE OF REHEARSALS

From the perspective of the trainee, rehearsal:

- helps build familiarity;
- provides an opportunity to iron out mistakes;
- allows time and space to try new actions at a pace which that individual can absorb;
- helps build confidence by mastering a new skill.

For the organization, rehearsal:

- reduces the chances of expensive and damaging mistakes in the field;
- shows which trainees look most capable;
- provides an opportunity to analyse and correct what might be going wrong and what could be done better;
- allows the trainer to comment and influence in (relative) privacy – this being an under-rated, yet effective and quiet way of achieving rapid changes.

Prototypes are usually tested in a laboratory or design studio, and then introduced gradually to the market in product form. Similarly, organizations can benefit from preparatory work on the impacts which their staff are likely to make on their behalf.

'Rehearsing' includes a range of practices from short, simple role-plays to complex, elaborate simulations.

SINK OR SWIM?

Some delegates are wary of role-play, whether through hearsay, bad experiences, or because they imagine that they will be made to look silly. They might prefer a simulation in which they are 'themselves' in a scenario which is as realistic as possible.

There is value in either approach. Sometimes it is useful to simulate work circumstances, sometimes pure exercises are needed, so that one particular element may be abstracted for polishing.

Encourage the wary participant to benefit from the 'facet-by-facet' method by stressing the clear measures of accomplishment which rehearsals can provide. Pilots progress from simulator to flying a plane and finally flying with passengers.

Remind trainees that role-play is real play, and they are capable of lending themselves to an exercise just as they might lend themselves to the 'role' for which they are employed – when, for example, dealing with customers.

There is room within inspirational training for several philosophies, which include the 'shallow end', the 'deep end' and the 'arm-bands'.

The **'deep end'** approach – 'You have to do it some time, it may as well be now' – has the virtue of making the big picture extremely clear, as the protagonist tries the whole task at once, right at the start of the learning process.

In my first few days as a trainee journalist, I had to interview real people involved in real news stories. If the resultant story was good enough, it would go into the newspaper. The experience was invaluable, and it is hard to imagine a simulation capturing the same degree of verisimilitude. Colleagues have spoken of the unforgettable impacts of making their first cold call, speech or stock purchase. In the right circumstances, this method works for many people. The danger is that if things go wrong, they may never want to try again. In the deep end, it is 'sink or swim', and not every organization can afford to drown too many new recruits.

The **'arm-band'** is a useful variant. Trainees are accompanied by someone experienced, without risking damage to themselves or to the relationship with the client. Experience is seen as essential ballast for youthful enthusiasm. Almost every American police film has a scene in which the rookie partners the senior officer – and nearly gets into trouble. (This is usually followed by extensive training in the shooting gallery!)

The **'shallow end'** consists of delegating only the easiest tasks until the trainee is entirely comfortable with them. Eventually, learners pluck up enough courage to venture beyond their depth. The question is whether the metaphor reflects reality in its implication of a point at which there is a real shift from 'foot on the floor' to 'swimming'. The answer depends on the particular activity – and in swimming at least we know there is such a divide. My opinion is that, for many people, comfortable familiarity with 'shallow ends' is good preparation for greater rigours to follow. In the training room, we can leave the shallow end quite swiftly by making any rehearsal as much like the critical aspects of a performance as possible.

FORUM REHEARSAL

A forum-style rehearsal reaches the heart of training and organizational issues, stretching beyond traditional role-play by:

- having performers play themselves;
- following a structure in which contributions for improvement are solicited during the action from highly-involved spectators;

- putting emphasis on 'personas' – for example, by asking people to find the part of themselves which enjoys platform performing.

The method has much in common with the Forum Theatre originated by the director Augusto Boal as one strand of his politically-inspired Theatre of the Oppressed. I have designed Rehearsal for Success sessions for trainers to lead groups through any process with a number of significant steps. They work for launching new products, services, or initiatives; for developing and practising new skills (including negotiating, leading a team and selling), and for the creation and exploration of strategic scenarios, such as planning futures for departments or entire organizations.

We create a live case study, which gives the participants the chance to expand their thinking. In a safe environment, delegates explore methods, suggest improvements, hear the other side and experiment with new approaches. They have the opportunity to overcome inhibitions, obstacles and objections.

Set up a Rehearsal for Success when you want to:

- explore winning behaviours;
- communicate with instant feedback;
- concentrate on the moments that matter;
- practise making perfect.

To start, find out what the group is rehearsing for. The briefing is either the first part of the session or is done in advance. You need to know the nature of the task – whether it is to launch the new product, apply an appraisal system or clinch a deal. Rehearsal for Success is appropriate when the desired outcomes are clear and interest lies in the human processes needed to reach those outcomes.

Ask everyone to sit in a semi-circle or horseshoe to begin. Scatter a few chairs at the front, which will become the focal point and performing area. You take the lead at the beginning, but with the aim of stepping aside soon in order to facilitate the process from the edges. Viola Spolin (1963) calls this 'side-coaching', a term which captures its essence. When side-coaching, the trainer assists players by reminding them where to place their attention. If everything is on track, there is no need to say anything. The trainer intervenes as little as possible, preferably without stopping the action. Instructions such as 'Remember what you want from him' or 'Mention the percentage now' would be typical.

The cases begin

Case rehearsals

First, the briefing. Ask your client to state the process which you are about to explore. Examples might be:

- 'We are launching a new medical product from our American suppliers, and need to introduce and sell it to the consultants in hospitals who are our buyers.'
- 'We are about to enter a critical negotiation with a major client, and must handle it successfully if the company is to survive.'
- 'We are going to expand the number of volunteer groups in our charity, and as professional leaders need to ensure that the working relationship is properly balanced.'

I shall refer to these case studies in *medical sales*, *negotiation* and *volunteer groups* to illustrate the principles below.

Not every client immediately expresses their situation with this degree of clarity. Help delegates to shape the description. If this proves problematic, it may be more useful to use another rehearsal format – such as Before and After semi-improvised scenes (see Variations, below).

Ask the group how their work process begins. What is the first significant event in the launch cycle, merger or expansion?

Let's say that, for the new medical product, it is a letter from America, explaining the launch. The client states that the important point for her assembled colleagues is to sell the new item to hospital consultants. Everything up to this point is now taken as given: the product has to be launched as developed, there is a timetable for doing so, and deliveries are expected at their usual regular intervals.

To ensure clarity, you might ask the recipient of the letter to read it aloud. They don't need the actual letter with them. From memory, they outline the salient detail, imagining that they are at their desk receiving it for the first time: 'Dear Managing Director, As you'll remember from our last conference, we are now launching the SuperProbe. Please confirm the sales targets from the chart below'.

You give the managing director an opportunity to recreate her immediate emotional and practical responses, reconstructed from the time the letter arrived, or – if she knows it is coming but has not yet arrived – how she imagines she will respond.

'It's fine. Pretty much what we were expecting, an ambitious target, but we can do it. Besides, we've no choice but to go for it,' she says, 'the first thing I do with this is confirm the details with America.'

As the facilitator, you probably guess that confirmation details are not germane to the training needs of the sales group, so you would tell the MD to assume that this has been done, and ask how she communicates the information to staff. You then cut the rehearsal to the next significant point. She responds, 'It could be by letter or could be at a regular team briefing'.

The MD is now generalizing, and we can accommodate both routine processes and interesting exceptions – perhaps by enacting both the letter 'route' and the team briefing strand until one reaches its conclusion or they meet again at a subsequent junction. Since, as far as possible, you let the client group determine the course of action, you might ask, 'Which would you prefer?'.

The MD says, 'I'll do both'. This provokes laughter from the team, and one of them says, 'Good, because when it's just by letter, nothing happens. It's only at the briefings that we find out what's really important and what's actually going on'.

Laughter early in a rehearsal often indicates recognition of reality. You ask, 'Do you need a letter at all?'. The MD replies, 'Yes, because we're all geographically spread out, and it's hard to meet more than once every six months'. And the colleague adds, 'The letter is good for confirmation and for reference. But we could do with more meetings, in my opinion'. The buzz of agreement prompts the MD to make a note to review the frequency of meetings.

It is now appropriate to cut to the meeting, deal with any communication difficulties that arise here, and so on for each significant step towards their goal. In the medical sales case, these are making the appointments, tracking the progress of the sales team and negotiating price details with America.

Our choices here depend primarily on time, but also on how many people will be interested and have valid contributions to make.

Guidelines for facilitating rehearsals

Principles to keep in mind throughout are as follows:

- **Participants should show – rather than tell.**
  The heart of the format is a drama. Explanations, justifications, excuses and theorizing should be kept to a minimum. The rehearsal is a doing event, which may be alternated with reflection and discussion time. As a guide, allow only sufficient debate to reach a decision on what to do next. Then insist that the decision is enacted. If it is difficult to resolve, enact more than one option to discover which works best.

  Suppose that one of the sales team says, 'I'd arrange a meeting with the consultant – which is not always that easy', and colleagues nod and give verbal agreement. Rather than allow a discussion of the difficulties – 'I'd ring up, and make an appointment', 'I'd insist he sees me', which are mere telling – dramatize them by saying 'Let's do it'.

  In the medical product rehearsal, the saleswoman – Annie – is setting up a meeting with a consultant surgeon. Annie acts out her own part, and volunteers play anyone who cannot be present. These other players might be drawn from other members of the sales force, who know what is said and done in the circumstances from their own experience, or might be actors brought in to play selected parts – such as the surgeon – with the advantage of being unknown to the protagonists. Players within the team are usually more than competent at playing all the characters, and 'unreality' is rarely an issue.

  For telephone calls, ask the two speakers to face away from each other and to mime a phone with their hands. Appropriate props can also be helpful here.

  The surgeon's secretary takes the call. The secretary is played by another saleswoman – Joan – who uses the opportunity to demonstrate one of the frustrating barriers she has so often encountered:

  'I'm sorry, Mr Stebbings won't be able to see you.'

  Annie responds, 'Oh! Why is that?'.

  'He's too busy. Goodbye.' And Joan mimes putting down the telephone.

  You tell Annie that she is still committed to arranging a meeting and ask what she is going to do. She says she will write to Stebbings, sending a brochure illustrating the benefits of the new product.

  As facilitator you sense that, while the letter has a chance of being effective, there's a disappointment that the telephone call failed to establish a meeting, so you ask, 'Can anyone suggest how a call might be handled differently, to get a meeting faster than the letter?'.

- **Seek better ideas, and allow the holder of the alternative idea to demonstrate.**

  If someone in a scene seems to be falling short of the best possible way of handling a situation (and it is one which matters), solicit a better idea. First allow the same player to make simple adjustments ('try saying "please" when requesting sugar in your coffee'). For more elaborate changes in tactics you have the option of swapping the players round. See if the suggester will take the place of the original player to demonstrate the tactics in mind. We are then back with showing rather than telling.

  If someone has a particular reason for wanting something done differently, then they may occupy the place to show the difference. . .

  'Yes', says Linda. 'Don't give the secretary the chance to close the conversation that easily.' You thank Annie, and invite Linda to take Annie's place and show what she means.

  Linda turns away from Joan and makes the call. 'I'd like to arrange a meeting with Mr Stebbings please.'

  'I'm sorry, he's too busy to see you.'

  'I appreciate that Mr Stebbings is a very busy man. I promise not to take up much of his time. In fact, I know he likes to see me and is keen to find out more about our new products, which is why we have regularly met every six months for the past couple of years. When would be the best date?'

  'I'll ask him. Can I come back to you?'

  'Do you have his diary?'

  'Er, yes.' Joan has to tell the truth of the situation as she knows it.

  'Well, let's pencil me in for the next mutually convenient half-hour, and we can confirm later.'

- **Allow a variety of approaches, and appreciate all efforts.**

  Remember to thank each player for their contribution. If you switch people around, explain that it is not because anyone went wrong, it's because we are using the forum to try various approaches. Later there may be benefits in making judgements about what works best. For now, we are putting strategies into action. To keep the action going fruitfully, you need players willing to participate, and that means they shouldn't feel judged. You are aiming for an atmosphere of experimentation, honest inquiry and discovery.

  In the volunteer groups case, the briefing made it plain that these groups were falling apart too frequently, meaning that the professional workers were either spending a great deal of time setting up replacement groups of volunteers or struggling to prevent their fragmentation.

  When scenes were played out between a professional coordinator and his volunteer group, we heard several complaints about a lack of back-up from head office. The group asked their paid coordinator for materials for a campaign, and he wanted to provide it. But head office would then refuse supplies.

In the rehearsal, Jim happened to be the only representative from head office. Everyone else was based in regional offices. Given our findings so far, the danger was that Jim would face much opposition and become upset or defensive – perfectly acceptable if our focus was dealing with complaints. But the selected issue was building better relationships between paid workers and volunteer groups, and it would be counter-productive to overburden Jim (who wasn't directly responsible for the supply system anyway). We needed his knowledge to provide authentic responses to hypothetical requests.

What happens, then, is that Jim (playing a variety of roles of head office personnel) states the genuine response – 'We can't give those posters to volunteers' – and handles the request as graciously as he can muster. We support him by asking if anyone has helpful suggestions.

If someone then steps into a head office role and says, 'Yes, you most certainly can have them', we know that they have overstepped the limits of the current system. These posters are not available. However, if someone says 'Sorry, no posters, but we do have campaign packs allocated for just such a group as yours. And I'll make sure they are with you by next week', then Jim may pick up a learning point for next time he's asked for posters. He also comes to understand the depth of feeling about each issue without having complaints aimed directly at him. What, to Jim, was previously the occasional request for posters for groups that weren't supposed to have them is now revealed as a significant barrier to the development of relationships between volunteers and their leaders.

He may even return to the rehearsal to take the call again, explaining the situation and adding, 'And I'll be asking the next management committee meeting to make posters available to volunteer groups as soon as possible'.

Whether his initiative eventually succeeds or not, the group leaders immediately understand his position and appreciate his efforts to help with their duties.

- **Aim to involve everyone at least once.**
In the negotiation rehearsal, all the staff of a small public relations company were preparing for a critical new deal with their principal client.

The team included a new employee, Ellen, who knew nothing of the background other than what she was hearing during the session. Invited at one point to swap with someone, she refused, saying she wouldn't know what to do. For the moment, we allowed her to remain in the audience. Later, as the negotiation reached its conclusion, we asked Ellen to take her place as the person who happened to pick up the call when the client telephoned to say he was accepting the offer.

We stipulated that no one else was in the office at the time. Ellen took the call, and dealt with it competently, thanking the client, and taking the initiative to ask for confirmation in writing. This gained her a round of applause from her new colleagues.

- **Side-coach by means of simple, direct calling in the form of instructions.**

In Rehearsals for Success, keep the action buoyant and set up opportunities for learning through doing. As Spolin (1963) puts it: 'Side-coaching keeps the stage space alive. . . It is the voice of the director seeing the needs of the over-all presentation; at the same time it is the voice of the teacher seeing the individual actor and his needs within the group and on the stage'. In other words, we can help someone who is stuck. Give them a simple instruction: 'Make that phone call now', 'Say goodbye – the meeting is over', or gesture for someone else to offer a suggestion or change roles.

When nothing significant seems to be happening, give the instruction to fast-forward to the next meeting, telephone call or whatever.

- **Trust your instincts.**

Cast the characters as your instinct suggests. While you will mostly ask people to play themselves, sometimes everyone gains by a swap: the protagonist will enjoy watching how someone else handles their struggles. Or you might ask them to play the other character in the scene – the buyer, the other negotiator, for example – and experience it from their standpoint. Swapping roles is a rich source of insight.

- **Bring it to a conclusion.**

Make sure the story is rounded off. How many scenes do you need? It may just be one or two, or it could be a dozen. It depends entirely on how many significant points or critical moments the process reveals. Judge progress as it goes along, trusting that you and the group have the resources to bring matters to a conclusion. This does not, however, mean that everything needs to be acted or that all problems will be solved – often the rehearsal reveals issues which cannot be resolved immediately because they involve people not present, for example.

If you feel at some point that the group has broken the back of the problem, then advance to the ending as swiftly as possible. For instance, say to the volunteer workers, 'You have dealt with the hardest parts. Time is short, so let's finish by enacting the six-monthly routine check meeting of the professional worker and his group, and finds out what's happening now.'

The players sit round the table, and the paid worker begins: 'Hi, everyone, good to see you. Thanks for the agenda you sent me, which looks great. Here's the box of materials you asked for. And there's a couple of new posters which we thought you might like. How are things going?'.

'It's all going well. We appreciated your call last week, and our campaigns are running smoothly. Let's crack on with plans for the next couple of street collections and the big meeting in Shrewsbury. . .'

At this point you intervene with, 'It's going well, let's stop there and imagine everyone blissfully walking hand-in-hand into the sunset. You've worked through the main issues in here, and we've all observed how you might go about things. Thank you for your ideas, your acting and your application to the key questions. Jot down any notes that are going to be useful to you'.

- **Use variations for more effective rehearsals.**
  Rehearsal is a flexible format. There are many variations. You may decide to play certain scenes in real time or allow time-outs for consultation. You could use professional actors as role-players. You could run the rehearsal with an audience.

  Given space, it is possible to play more than one scene at a time, creating a more complex simulation.

  A useful variant for simplifying complex change questions is to have participants play two scenes, one showing how things are now, and the other how they would be after the change, with everything running perfectly. The 'before' and 'after' scenes create dramatic contrast and vividly illustrate the goal. By enacting the desired scenario, participants often identify the first steps towards a change.

NEW REALITIES

At their heart, rehearsals concern experiencing and creating new realities. You are working with strategies and skills which managers can learn from actors. In rehearsal, actors familiarize themselves with the process of manufacturing reality. They repeatedly live out situations which they invent on the spot. Yet the made-up emotions and beliefs are experienced and played as everyday reality.

Rehearsal processes allow everyone to play with creating realities, learn to enjoy the beliefs, emotions and images that arise, and select those which they wish to make manifest in the outside world.

Rehearsals produce clear expositions of team members' situations. Guided practice of what everyone needs to do means that trainees are ready for key moments when they occur within work settings. And in each of the cases described above, the rehearsal led to success.

⑥
■NSPIRATIONS

- Use the CEA strategy to dispel any fears associated with dealing with questions.
- As you gain confidence, rehearsals can combine your spontaneity with that of your participants to spectacular, inspirational effect.
- Allow participants to reach their own solutions: solo; with help from colleagues; with help from you.
- Trust your instincts and trust the process you have chosen.

12

Endings

Complete the learning cycle in a satisfying way by deriving your own lessons from the programmes you run, as you consider the future of training – and your part in it.

Endings – like beginnings – are memorable. I recall very little about a concert I attended long ago by the ex-Monkee Mike Nesmith. But I do remember the ending. He said we should show our appreciation by allowing the performance to finish with silence instead of applause. The audience respected his wishes, and as he laid down his guitar, we quietly left. This provided a stunning contrast to all the other music shows I was familiar with, where the impact was assumed to tally with the number of encores and standing ovations.

ANY OTHER BUSINESS?

To complete the learning, your sessions need to join up two fundamental threads – the content and the process. During the programme you will have opened up a variety of topics, aired new ideas and begun rehearsals. If it is the sort of event where many possibilities are floated – perhaps a seminar on the future of an organization – participants may need to make selections and decisions. Even with less open structures, trainees will benefit from recaps and reviews, to ensure that content has been covered and absorbed.

They will also expect a psychological completion, where the things that need to be said between people can be said, and what needs to be done is given due time and space. Participants require this kind of closure to feel satisfied by a programme. They may, for example, need to be acknowledged for their efforts and commitment. They may wish to acknowledge the teacher and/or each other.

You can ask explicitly as you approach the end of a session or course, 'What else do we need to do?' and be fairly certain that anything sufficiently important will be mentioned. With flexibility, you can incorporate the requests, or at least make it clear that certain aspects are outside the immediate scope and will not be dealt with. Nothing need be left unknowingly hanging.

COMPLETION

ACTIVITY

End circle

A simple, satisfying completion routine is to draw everyone into a circle, and announce that you are going to end by following a certain procedure.

The circle and statement create a feeling of ritual, which operates on the visceral level. Humans crave appropriate completions, and we should supply them if we have worked with any intensity with a group for a day or more.

Each person in turn has the opportunity to speak to resolve any outstanding matters. This might consist of two points, perhaps with a time limit. For example, each person can select one action point to announce to the circle, and can say anything they want to say to the people with whom they have been sharing the course: 'On Monday, I shall meet my manager and ask for clear guidance regarding the division of responsibilities. And I'd like to say it's been a pleasure to meet all of you, and to discover that what I thought were very individual problems are in fact common to most of us'.

Thank the speaker, taking care not to comment on what they have said or to open a general discussion. Form is at the heart of ritual, and it would be inappropriate to review the course itself at this point. If anyone begins to do so, remind them that the comments are to say what they need to say to the other participants. The reviewing can take place in other formats later.

When everyone, including yourself, has spoken (and one of the advantages of a circle is that no one need notice that the trainer speaks first and last), announce that the course is now formally complete.

A variant – and each trainer has a preferred way of finishing – is for each participant to summarize in one word or phrase 'our time together', to state one thing they have learnt, and to reveal what they would say to anyone proposing to attend the programme in future.

CERTIFICATES

Successful participants may receive a certificate. If a course is part of a recognized programme, the award of a diploma – for completion or after passing a test – is usually built in.

For your own courses or company courses, you can probably choose. But are certificates worth the bother? Can something essentially decorative make a difference for the trainer who wants to get the best from trainees? After all, the course has ended, and either the participants have done the work or they haven't, and by that point a certificate will make no difference. The answer is that anyone completing a programme is likely to enjoy receiving a certificate. It serves as a recognition that they have done the requisite work, which in turn could contribute towards an award or further qualification.

More subtly, a diploma serves as a reminder and validation of what has taken place. By triggering memories, the certificate can help to keep the messages of a programme alive long after is has finished. Each time a graduate sees the certificate, it can prompt memories, states and behaviours which reinforce learning. In a work file, on an office wall or dusted down for the right occasion, it serves as proof to the holder and evidence to the outside world.

You might also find it helpful to use the promise of a certificate as a motivator. Mention it early, show how attractive and imposing it looks, and some participants may even work towards the diploma as a goal in itself. It concentrates minds on completing a course, as its award clearly depends on getting to the end.

An additional benefit is that an attractive certificate might win display in all sorts of places, advertising your courses and services, and encouraging more people to attempt to join the roll of honour.

Who should receive the certificate? This may be anyone who has completed the course, or anyone who has demonstrated the required competence – preferably by showing their learning as part of the programme's activities.

REVIEW TO IMPROVE

Companies expect their training to be value for money, and many now use a four-level evaluation model (usually derived from the work of Donald Kirkpatrick), which helps the aware trainer to shape the programme.

Evaluation considers:

- how participants reacted to the course, testing immediate impressions about content, the trainer, the venue;

- what people have learnt as a result of the training;
- what behaviour changes the training has made (usually when the learner returns to the workplace);
- what benefits have been gained by the learner's department or organization.

As you go down the list, the impacts are harder to influence and more difficult to measure. Nevertheless, these are the areas to target, particularly if you can find ways of demonstrating the contribution your training has made.

The most important areas of immediate evaluation at the end of a programme are to: **review the event for ourselves** so that we can improve what we do; and **follow-up with the client** to obtain customer feedback as a source of further information and to improve the prospects of keeping that customer satisfied.

It is good discipline to keep notes of how you can improve your work. Any time an idea occurs to you, jot it down so it can be reviewed at the end of the programme. Some notions which seemed a good idea at the time will have lost their lustre when you review; others will still look like real improvements and can be incorporated into the design and future runnings.

You might set the review process as a personal challenge. How can you make at least one significant improvement each time you run a session or event? End-of-session reviews with participants often provide useful information, and your own instincts will generate awareness of where change would be helpful.

Some ideas will be easy to implement. Others may seem trickier. Attending other trainers' sessions, whether as guest observer or full participant, can be a good way of filling any skill gaps. Then you also benefit from picking up new ideas, through copying methods used by excellent trainers and – subject to copyright laws – borrowing activities, processes and concepts.

While core principles retain their validity, styles sometimes change rapidly, and new information constantly comes on stream for all subjects. Attending courses helps keep us up to date and well informed.

The other strand is follow-up with the client. This may be a simple telephone call to request feedback, or it may involve a more rigorous, statistically-based follow-up with forms and questionnaires. It depends what you want to know and how much the client can reasonably tell.

External consultants derive extra benefit from written comments. These create a record of work delivered and, with permission, make valuable testimonials when canvassing for new projects.

Even internal consultants and trainers are involved in marketing and, when a project goes well, can take the opportunity to find out what else the satisfied customers – sponsoring manager or participants – will want. Key questions include 'How can this programme be improved for future participants?' and 'What other services are you seeking?' It then makes a telling marketing point to inform clients about improvements in existing products and to introduce new programmes to meet their stated needs.

MEASURES OF SUCCESS

Training and teaching have become commodities, bought and sold on the market. The values of the marketplace create many absurdities, one of these being that we often pay trainers and teachers less than other professionals. This has resulted in a down-grading of these professions.

Just as quality in parenting or in community spirit cannot be bought, so training and teaching – defined as bringing out the best from people by enabling them to learn – are essentially unquantifiable.

Because the market has its place, the worth of trainers has to be shown in measurable terms too, and there are many ways of doing this. Yet whatever measurements are chosen will carry judgements of value. The value might be monetary. To take a simple example: a company may invest £5000 in a training programme, aimed at improving employees' telephone skills. If telephone sales increase over the next quarter by £10,000, the course was clearly worthwhile financially.

But even this eminently positive example is not so straightforward. We are not dealing with a scientific experiment, with proper controls and isolated variables. All sorts of factors may have contributed to the increased sales – perhaps some customers just happened to have more money to spend. Nonetheless, someone will make a judgement, and will probably attribute the added value entirely or largely to the training.

The founding fathers of NLP, Richard Bandler and John Grinder, write interestingly about the scientific model (1990: 167):

> ... it says 'In a complex system, the one way to find out something about it scientifically is to restrict everything in the situation except one variable. Then you change the value of that variable and notice any changes in the system.' I think that's an excellent way to figure out cause-effect relationships in the world of experience. I do not think it is a useful model in face-to-face communication with another human being who is trying to get a change.

Rather than restrict all behaviour in a face-to-face communication, you want to vary your behaviour wildly, to do whatever you need to do in order to elicit the response that you want.

Learning is not primarily a scientific process. The presence of evaluations, measurements and precise objectives may make learning (and training) look scientific. But besides delivering important content and factual data, the process of training is an art, encompassing intuitions, impressions, perceptions and personal chemistry. We seek results and they are more likely to come through inspiration and insight than rote.

Let us consider a looser model for measuring value and success. Suppose a company identifies a training need and, after your training programme, you deliver a group of people each exhibiting the required skills. Your job is done, and the measurement is the ability of those people to exhibit the skills (which they then have to put into practice to make any impact on their organizations). The organization approves of these results, because they contribute to its aims, either in relatively precise terms such as numerical targets, or non-numerical ones such as improved atmospheres. If a programme is designed to improve teamwork or communication, measurements of success can vary from quantifiable outputs made by the team (car production up by 20 per cent this week), or by individuals in the team ('Jack is pressing two more bodies per day'), through to impressionistic judgements ('the atmosphere has improved considerably, and the plant is buzzing'). Non-numeric outcomes are as valid as numeric and, in training contexts, are often more significant.

Sometimes the harder-to-measure results of training programmes are undervalued. They are said to be in the realm called 'soft skills', or they are dismissed with phrases like 'touchy-feely'. What lies behind this disparagement is either the placing of low value on feelings or the lazily reductive practice of only valuing what can be measured numerically. While some organizations may function without contact or emotion, they will fall behind those which value their human resources. As psychologist Abraham Maslow puts it, 'Many things are called weak which we are learning are not weak at all'.

While trainers may need to persuade organizations to fund their activities, providing value is the central purpose of their work – not demonstrating it.

CHANGE AND THE INCREASING IMPORTANCE OF LEARNING

Organizations are keen to shape our beliefs and change our awareness of the world. This is the very stuff of marketing, branding and advertising. When revealing the inner workings of influence and choice, trainers strengthen people's abilities to understand and deal in these dimensions.

Successful training pivots on change, and improvisational learning methods have the power to transform rigid beliefs, thoughts and behaviours into flexibility, spontaneity and creativity. Psychologist David Lewis writes:

> When a particular mind set becomes rigid and impermeable to change, it leads to stereotyped thinking. A highly prejudiced person, for example, focuses very narrowly on any information that seems to support his bigotry, while refusing to perceive anything that might challenge those perceptions. In other words, he sees what he expects to see.

One morning my neighbour's car wouldn't start, because it was a cold day and his battery was low. I helped him to push-start it. Immediately afterwards, my car wouldn't start, and I assumed the problem was the same. In fact, the automatic gear happened to be out of the 'Park' position, which is the only one in which the engine responds. Even though I 'knew' that a low battery would have made some sound, the silence didn't snap me out of my prejudice. I started cursing and worrying about reaching my destination. Luckily my passenger pointed to the solution – she knew nothing about the neighbour, and just enough about starting a car.

How we behave depends on what state we are in. And we can put ourselves into resourceful or unresourceful states. If we lose our way, help from someone else often puts us back into a resourceful state. As personal development guru Anthony Robbins (1988: 64) writes: 'Belief is nothing but a state, an internal representation that governs behaviour'. We can choose beliefs conducive to success or to failure, to learning or not learning. And we can learn how to learn.

Sometimes people change because insight strikes in an instant. Conditions alter: something snaps or shifts and change becomes possible and inevitable. At other times we evolve or transform. Each step is apparent and the links are clear. Sometimes we change, but hardly notice it at all. It is gradual, evolutionary and subtle.

Windy Dryden and Jack Gordon (1996) write: 'Thinking, feeling and behaving are all inter-related. . . we have emphasized that if you wish to effect a deep philosophic change at either the specific or general level towards a more rational view of life, you had better employ a battery of methods designed to encourage not only more rational ways of thinking, but also more appropriate ways of feeling and behaving'. You might also be familiar with a cycle of change, in which you learn the same lessons again and again, but each time at different, 'deeper' levels as you become ready for them.

During the processes of inspirational training, your clients will experience all types of change, and you should stay alert to every possibility, developing a sense of what sort of changes are most likely to be encouraged by which techniques.

The assumption that change will take place is one of the cornerstones of solution-focused therapy, a system of thought which could have a massive impact on organizations. Solution-focused practitioners believe that once an action has started it tends to continue – which we might call the inertia effect – and that positive deeds are the upshot of hope and expectancy. When a trainer assumes change in the desired direction, the client is drawn into sharing the assumption, and actions will follow. Although these may be small actions to begin with, they will affect the whole system.

The initial changes needn't even have anything to do with the causes of a problem. In many cases, all the obvious means of attacking the problem directly will already have been tried and failed. A different approach is needed.

A mother of a 'delinquent' son often claims to have 'tried everything' to control his behaviour. What she perhaps hasn't tried is a word of praise for something he is doing right, or introducing good times into the daily routine.

When a small step shows promise, the prescription is to carry on doing it. Practice leads to perfection, and the client is increasingly empowered to make changes. Whether in therapeutic or organizational contexts, the client is encouraged to draw on existing resources and to act as if the desired goals are already being achieved. A significant part of the trainer's role is to catch people doing things right. When these things are duly mentioned or complimented, more and more of the resources are utilized.

If a team has been working well below potential, with factions or squabbling, for example, help create a scenario of how it would be if the team were working together at their best. From this picture, the group might set goals. But rather than aim directly for lofty goals – which might be described by the team as the results of 'a miracle having occurred' – set a small task as the first step. In this instance it might be for each member to notice the positive qualities of the others during the next week.

By carrying out the simple task, team members will be learning the valuable skill of observing talents of others – which is doing something quite different from most people's normal practice, which is to look for (and therefore find and be conditioned by) limitations.

At the next session, compliment them on the observations they have made. Try a circle exercise to capitalize on their groundwork. Each member takes a turn to say what he or she likes or appreciates about each of the others. A variant is for each member to state what he or she would miss if no longer part of the team.

Because solution-focused practice assumes that participants have the resources for the changes they wish to make, it calls for restraint from the trainer. In assessments, for example, take care to avoid undeserved praise or frequent unnecessary judgement, which diminishes confidence. Participants can assess themselves, perhaps measuring their own progress along scales of 0–10, where 10 represents them at their very best.

FREEDOM AND STRUCTURE

When managers are under pressure, traditional remedies for stress involve relaxation (and similar techniques). In fact, confidence to improvise is a more powerful resource available to managers for dealing with many of the other demands they face. From a foundation of confidence, anyone can gain the power to act with greater spontaneity, adaptability and creativity – to their own advantage and that of their organization.

Life sciences tell us that the most advantageous environment for living systems to operate is at 'the edge of chaos', defined at the microscopic level of chemical bonding as the point between solid and liquid. Here structures exist in a slowly flowing state, free to change continuously but without losing their underlying structure. At the interface between freedom and structure you experience the best of both worlds. If the environment is frozen, there is too little latitude for change. If there is chaos, one change could create uncontrollable change elsewhere.

In human bodies, living muscle – which gives us our physical flexibility – is stretchy, ductile and has a consistency not much thicker than spittle. Bones give us our structure, and from our brains come the messages which drive changes. Brain power has long been replacing muscle power as a passport to human 'success', and in particular success derives from knowing how to acquire and deal with information.

Successful teaching and training harness all the resources that trainees possess. Ideally, they provide those conditions which stimulate the natural desire to learn, and furnish generative techniques and tools for learning to continue after the class has ended.

As you use the powerful tools of inspirational training to empower people and help them discover their own talents, so you will inevitably be enhancing your own creativity in all areas of your life and work.

NSPIRATIONS

- Offer participants psychological completion of a training pro-
gramme to send them on their way both satisfied and inspired.
- They might also appreciate a certificate.
- Review the programme to improve it for next time – checking both
contents and processes.
- Seek solutions rather than limitations.
- Stay in the complex interface between solid structure and chaos.

And some words of wisdom from a pair of sages, ancient and more
modern:

'Do not confine your children to your own learning, for they were
born in a different time.'

Ancient Hebrew proverb

'If there's anything in my show which you haven't understood, please
consider it significant.'

Scottish comedian Arnold Brown

References

Alon, R (1996) *Mindful Spontaneity: Lessons in the Feldenkrais method*, North Atlantic Books, Berkeley, CA.

Bandler, R and Grinder, J (1990) *Frogs into Princes*, Eden Grove Editions, London

Browning, R (1845) *Andrea de Santo*

Buzan, T (1974, revised 1989) *Use Your Head*, BBC Publications, London

Campbell, L, Campbell, B and Dickinson, D (1995) *Teaching and Learning through Multiple Intelligences*, 2nd edn, Prentice-Hall, Englewood Cliffs, NJ

Carlzon, J (1987) *Moments of Truth*, HarperCollins, London

Carse, J P (1986) *Finite and Infinite Games*, Ballantine, London

Case, J, quoted in *Professional Manager* May 1996

Covey, S (1992) *The Seven Habits of Highly Effective People*, Simon & Schuster, Hemel Hempstead

Dennison, P E and Dennison G E (1988), *Brain Gym*, Edu-Kinesthetics, Ventura, CA

Dryden, W and Gordon, J (1996) *Peak Performance: Become more effective at work*, Mercury, San Francisco, CA

Fritz, R (1989) *The Path of Least Resistance*, Fawcett Press, New York

Goleman, D (1996) *Emotional Intelligence*, Bloomsbury, London

Handy, C (1989) *The Age of Unreason*, Business Books, London

Johnstone, K (1981) *Impro*, Methuen, London

Lewis, D *Mind Skills*, Souvenir Press, London (currently out of print).

Lowen, A (1975) *Bioenergetics*, Penguin Books, Harmondsworth

McKellen, I (1993) quoted in *Independent on Sunday*, 23 June

Morgan, G (1993) *Imaginization: The art of creative imagination*, Sage Publications, Thousand Oaks, CA

Robbins, A (1988) *Unlimited Power*, Simon & Schuster, Hemel Hempstead

Rogers, C (1994) *Freedom to Learn*, Prentice-Hall, Englewood Cliffs, NJ

Rosenthal R and Jacobsen L F (1968) *Pygmalion in the Classroom*, Rinehart and Winston, New York

Sims Jr, H P and Lorenzi, P (1992), *The New Leadership Paradigm*, Sage Publications, London

Spolin, V (1983) *Improvisation for the Theatre*, Northwestern University Press, Evanston, IL

Wolfe, T (1979) *The Right Stuff*, Bantam Books, New York

Wurman, R S (1991) *Information Anxiety*, Pan, London

Zaporah, R (1995) *Action Theater: The improvisation of presence*, North Atlantic Books, Berkeley, CA

Further reading

These are some of the books that I've found useful while writing about inspirational training. The list may be exhausting, but is not of course exhaustive.

For a selection of training room layout diagrams, see *The Trainer's Pocketbook* (8th edn) by John Townsend, published in 1996 by Management Pocketbooks, Alresford, Hants (1-870471-37-7).

For handling emotion in groups, *The Small Group Trainer's Survival Guide* by Reichard, Siewers and Rodenhauser, published in 1992 by Sage Publications, London (0-8039-4757-7), is full of practical advice.

There are many books about NLP. *Unlimited Power* by Anthony Robbins, published in 1988 by Simon & Schuster, Hemel Hempstead (0-671-69976-8), is a readable, if lengthy, introduction to the principles, and is American enthusiast in style. Two aimed particularly at trainers are *The Excellent Trainer: Putting NLP to work* by Di Kamp, published in 1996 by Gower, Aldershot (0-566-07694-2), and *Training with NLP: Skills for managers, trainers and communicators* by Joseph O'Connor and John Seymour, published in 1994 by Thorsons, London (0-7225-2853-1). These apply all the NLP jargon at considerable length to the world of training. Then there's *Frogs into Princes* by Richard Bandler and John Grinder, published in 1990 by Eden Grove Editions (1-870845-03-X), which is a rich transcript of a sequence of NLP seminars.

The plentiful number of books about memory by Tony Buzan include *Use Your Head*, published by BBC Books, London in 1974, then revised in 1989 (0-563-20811-2).

Something of a rich, dense treatise for anyone fascinated by the philosophy of rules is *Finite and Infinite Games*, by James P Carse, published in 1986 by Ballantine, London, 180-345-34184-8.

You might be persuaded by *Persuading People, An Introduction to Rhetoric* by Robert and Susan Cockcroft, published in 1992 by Macmillan Press, Basingstoke (0-333-47163-6). Other useful presentation skill tomes are: *Successful Presentations for Dummies* by Malcolm Kushner, published in 1996 by IDG Books, New York; *How to overcome nervous tension and speak well in public* by Alfred Tack, published in 1955 by World's Work Ltd, Tadworth, Surrey (437-95152-9); and *Influence: Science and practice* by Robert B Cialdini, published in 1988 by HarperCollins, London (0-673-46751-1).

For mindmap information, there's Tony Buzan's colourful *The Mindmap Book*, published in 2000 by BBC Books, London (0-563-37101-3). Or try the set of audio tapes: Michael Gelb, *Mind Mapping*, published in the US by Nightingale Conant is full of useful tips, though it overstates its case by appearing to present mindmapping as the key to all the secrets of the universe. *The New Leadership Paradigm* by Henry P Sims Jr and Peter Lorenzi, published in 1992 by Sage Publications, London (0-8039-4298-2), is good on motivation and draws partly on E A Locke and G P Latham's *A Theory of Goal Setting and Task Performance*, published in 1990 by Prentice-Hall, Englewood Cliffs, NJ.

There is a mix of poetic and practical approaches to writing in Natalie Goldberg's *Writing Down The Bones*, published in 1988 by Shambhala, Boston and London (0-87773-375-9).

If you want to know more about brains and intelligence, dip into: *The Owner's Manual for the Brain* by Pierce J Howard, published in 1994 by Leornian Press, Austin, Texas (0-9636389-0-4) is stuffed with info and applications; *Teaching and Learning Through Multiple Intelligences* by Linda Campbell, Bruce Campbell and Dee Dickinson, currently published by Allyn and Baron, Needham Heights, MA – very accessible; and Ned Herrmann has his own system in *The Whole Brain Business Book*, published in 1996 by McGraw-Hill, New York (0-07-028462).

For a more technical summary of brain research, see the 4th edition of *Left Brain, Right Brain* by Springer and Deutsch, published in 1997 by W H Freeman and Co, New York (0-7167-2373-5).

To exercise brain and body: *Brain Gym for Business* by Dennison, Dennison and Teplitz, published in 1994 by Edu-Kinesthetics Inc, California (0-942143-03-5) and *Brain Gym* by Paul E and Gail E Dennison, published in 1988 by Edu-Kinesthetics, Ventura, California.

The Learning Revolution by Gordon Dryden and Jeanette Vos, published in 1994 by Accelerated Learning Systems Ltd, Aylesbury, Bucks (0-905553-43-8), is a terrific book on accelerated learning, with applications from childhood to dotage, taking in organizations along the way. *The Foreign Language Teacher's Suggestopedic Manual* by Georgi Lozanov and Evalina Gateva, published in 1988 by Gordon and Breach, New York, gives specific applications from the founders of a principal strand of accelerated learning.

Creative Visualisation by Ronald Shone, published in 1984 by Thorsons, Wellingborough (0-7225-0830-1), has all you need to know to develop your visualization skills, while *Emotional Intelligence* by Daniel Goleman, published in 1996 by Bloomsbury, London (0-7475-2830-6), offers a thorough exposition of the importance and impact of emotion on intelligence.

Information Anxiety by Richard Saul Wurman, published in 1991 by Pan, London (0-330-31097-6), elegantly puts the information explosion into reassuring perspective: 'Books are a major source of information anxiety, and I'd like to ensure that you won't feel anxious about reading this one'.

Bodywork books include: *The Alexander Principle* by Wilfred Barlow, published in 1973 by Victor Gollancz Ltd, London (0-575-04749-6) – one of several good introductions to the technique, covered here in ample detail; and *The Use of the Self* by F M Alexander, published in 1985 by Victor Gollancz Ltd, London (0-575-03720-2) – by the master himself.

Feldenkrais Method is richly explained through a mix of exercises and insightful commentary in *Mindful Spontaneity: Lessons in the Feldenkrais Method* by Ruthy Alon, published in 1996 by North Atlantic Books, Berkeley, California (1-55643-185-6).

Bioenergetics by Alexander Lowen, published in 1975 by Penguin, London (0-14-004322-5), offers a good introduction to Lowen's work, which stresses the emotional dimensions to any physical learning.

The spontaneity section is led by the classic *Impro* by Keith Johnstone, published in 1981 by Methuen, London (0-413-46430-X), and supplemented by the 20-day programme of *Action Theatre: The Improvisation of Presence* by Ruth Zaporah, published in 1995 by North Atlantic Books, Berkeley, California (1-55643-186-4). Both books are primarily about improvisation for theatrical purposes, but offer enough pointers in their principles and exercises for trainers to find inspiration for their own needs. *Drawing on the Right Side of the Brain* by Betty Edwards, published in 1993 by Harper-Collins, London (0-00-638114-6), is an inspiring selection of processes designed to 'unlock your hidden artistic talent'.

Inspiration from the arena of space flight abounds in *The Right Stuff* by Tom Wolfe, published in 1979 by Bantam Books, New York (0 553 17734 6).

There are more drama games in *Improvisation for the Theatre* by Viola Spolin, published in 1983 by Northwestern University Press, Illinois (0-8101-4000-4), and in *Games for Actors and Non-Actors* by Augusto Boal, published in 1992 by Routledge, London (0-415-06155-5), which has a strong political slant. Boal's philosophy is explored by his fellow practitioners in *Playing Boal: Theatre, therapy, activism*, edited by Schutzman and Cohen-Cruz, published in 1994 by Routledge, London (0-415-08608-6) – a mixed bag.

The Seven Habits of Highly Effective People by Stephen R Covey, published by Simon & Schuster (0-671-66398-4), is the cream of the self-improvement books, based on Covey's research into history of self-improvement/success literature and is a wise distillation, slightly infected by religious and prescriptive flavours. Liked by Bill Clinton.

The Path Of Least Resistance: Learning to become the creative force in your own life by Robert Fritz, published by Fawcett Press, New York (0-449-90337-0), is a strong, spirited, if overlong book on creativity. It has a great deal of theory with a personal rather than a business focus.

Training and Development Competence: A practical guide by Jill Brookes, published by Kogan Page, London (0-7494-1462-6), offers a thorough trek through competence-oriented training.

Mental disciplines can be enhanced using *Mind Skills* by David Lewis, published by Souvenir Press, London (0-285-62770-8), and *Peak Performance: Become more effective at work by* Windy Dryden and Jack Gordon, published by Mercury (1-85252-182-1).

Well-attuned books with a management perspective include *Managing Your Self: Management by detached involvement* by Jagdish Parikh in the 'Developmental Management' series published in 1993 by Blackwell Business (0-631-19307-3) – a good mix of esoteric and practical – and *Imaginization: The art of creative management* by Gareth Morgan, published by Sage Publications, London (0-8039-5299-6), which has lots of bizarre concepts and diagrams. This book provokes the imagination, but you need to do your own work to find its applications.

Finally, I like *Conceptual Blockbusting: A guide to better ideas* by James L Adams, a classic on thinking creatively, better ideas and problem-solving, with good summaries of previous efforts. The third edition was published in 1987 by Penguin, Harmondsworth (0-14-009842-91974).

Index

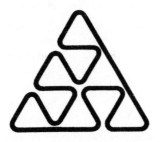